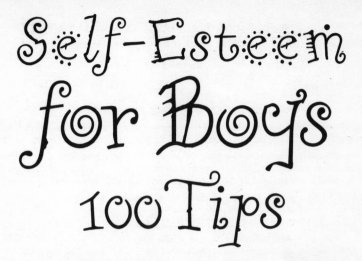

Self-Esteem
for Boys
100 Tips

for Raising Happy and
Confident Children

Elizabeth Hartley-Brewer

Vermilion
LONDON

DEDICATION

For my son, Stephen, and his constant friends Danny, Jonny, Pete, Dave, Greg, Richard and Paul, with whom he has shared so much for so long

9 10

Text copyright © 2000 by Elizabeth Hartley-Brewer

The right of Elizabeth Hartley-Brewer to be identified as the author of this work has been asserted by her in accordance with the Copyright, Designs and Patents Act, 1988.

First published in the United Kingdom in 2000 by Vermilion
an imprint of Ebury Press
Random House · 20 Vauxhall Bridge Road · London SW1V 2SA

Random House Australia (Pty) Limited
20 Alfred Street · Milsons Point · Sydney · New South Wales 2061 · Australia

Random House New Zealand Limited
18 Poland Road · Glenfield · Auckland 10 · New Zealand

Random House (Pty) Limited
Isle of Houghton · Corner of Boundary Road & Carse O'Gowrie
Houghton 2198 · South Africa

Random House Publishers India Private Limited
301 World Trade Tower · Hotel Intercontinental Grand Complex
Barakhamba Lane · New Delhi 110 001 · India

Random House UK Limited Reg. No. 954009

A CIP catalogue record for this book is available from the British Library

ISBN 9780091855871

Designed by Lovelock & Co.

Contents

Acknowledgments

As someone, clearly, with no direct experience of being male, I have had to check things out with a number of boys, and male friends and colleagues. I have also had help from teacher friends who work closely with boys – and girls – at the educational frontier to give them meaning, respect and personal fulfilment.

I should like, then, to thank Dexter Hutt, Principal of Ninestiles School in Birmingham and Gary Wilson, Head of English at Newsome High, Huddersfield, both of whom gave precious time to conversations and script reading, not to forget their children who had to do without their attention at these times. I should also like to thank Geoff Evans, of the C'mon Everybody project; George Hosking, who works with young violent men to help them understand and calm their souls; Adrienne Katz, who founded the research organisation 'Young Voice', through which growing boys and girls have been able to speak and be heard; Dr Sebastian Kraemer for sight of his paper, 'The Fragile Male', and for responding so promptly to my e-mails; and Joanne Edelman, friend and mother of two boisterous growing boys.

The idea for this book came from Jacqueline Burns, my editor. Had she not been such fun to work with, I would not have written it. I am very grateful to her, for I have learnt much in the process. Finally, I thank my son, Stephen. It has been a real privilege to be his mother. I wish him every happiness as he leaves his teens and embarks on adulthood.

CHAPTER 1

Understanding His Challenges and Opportunities

Boys are in the news as having a hard time at the moment. They seem to be struggling, finding it harder and harder to succeed, conform and find a comfortable role in life. Statistics tell us that boys experience more behavioural problems; get involved in more crime and at a younger age; are losing the academic edge they once held over girls; and demonstrate their despair in significantly higher suicide rates than girls. Social, economic and even educational changes seem to be undermining their essential manhood, and some see the future as promising little but constant pressure or failure, or both. Their self-esteem and motivation appear to be at rock bottom.

However, many boys continue to do exceptionally well and enjoy greater freedom, having thrown off the chains of only one vision of masculinity. They thrive on the challenge of living in this new world and find comfort in the permission to think, feel and act in tune with the warm heart within them.

Boys are lovable, amusing, destructive, proud and defiant and come in all possible shapes and sizes. Evidence is mounting that their brains as well as their bodies are different from girls'. It matters a very great deal how they grow up and how much respect society and families give them. It really matters, too, that they don't see education as an all-female province. It is crucial that they are allowed to respond to their male instincts within an understanding environment, so that they may feel true to themselves without following images of manhood that will lead them into trouble. Boys need just as much love, care and attention as girls in order to become lovable, loving, resilient and well-rounded adults who can make the most of life. Boys' positive self-esteem must derive not only from being happy to be male and having a clear idea of what manhood means, but also from a secure sense of who they are.

Boys are half our future. Given the changes taking place in society, particularly in employment and the family, growing boys will naturally feel confused and uncertain about the future. For instance, what does fatherhood mean? How important are commitment and marriage? How should they manage their sometimes contradictory feelings of sadness, anger, tenderness, competitiveness and protectiveness? Yet, while these changes may be unsettling, they are also potentially liberating, for they offer boys more ways of being themselves and thus of strengthening their self-esteem.

In future, parents and teachers may need to give boys more support and guidance as they navigate their way round the increasing choices facing them. Instead of being able to slip effortlessly into a pre-set stereotype, boys must look to what lies inside them and experiment with ways to express and develop the threads of self that are woven into the fabric of character. As self-knowledge increases, self-esteem deepens.

Boys now stand at a crossroad. They can choose a path leading to diminishing opportunities and greater self-doubt, or one towards self-development and deeper self-worth. Which route they choose will depend on the quality of their self-esteem.

When a boy has a good relationship with an adult who makes him feel understood, valued and wanted; when he feels supported so that he does well in school, becomes competent and confident; and, through his various interests, gains several reliable groups of friends with whom he learns to socialise and sort out differences, he learns to face the future with confidence and courage. It is vital for his mental health that he avoids becoming isolated and morose, for a world without others easily becomes peopled by demons.

Industrial buildings that house hazardous chemicals carry a warning sign on their walls. Parents should take equal heed when they see their son carrying a label with the three 'I's: 'Isolation', 'Insecurity' and 'Insignificance'. They are explosive, and create an emotional cocktail that can damage someone for a lifetime.

Internal strength is the antidote for these corrosives. In the past, boys had to toughen up emotionally and physically. Partly for survival on the battlefield, skins were thickened and upper lips stiffened, often through bullying, to condition men to hide feelings that could let their country down. Resilience is, undoubtedly, important, but boys – and girls too – also need to be flexible, to be able to regenerate themselves after setbacks, and to develop what we might call 'emotional courage'.

This does not mean denying feelings – far from it. Those who survive in the twenty-first century will have equipped themselves with sophisticated social and relationship skills. They will possess 'emotional literacy', to use a current popular term. Boys must learn how to be in touch with their own and others' feelings and perceptions because technological progress and greater global competition are creating jobs which require creative team work, collective problem-solving, constant communication and joint approaches to risk.

Parents and educators of boys today are challenged to present them with a comfortable male identity without the teflon armour that cuts them off from themselves and others. The non-stick, nonchalant world of macho culture gets males nowhere. Feelings and people should stick. By helping boys develop inner strength and nurturing their sometimes fragile self-esteem, we can help them to become happy, warm, generous, confident individuals, fathers and contributors to our society in the future – to everyone's benefit, including their own.

CHAPTER 2

Meeting His Needs

It is hard to accept that babies start off not knowing what sex they are. They experience themselves simply in terms of their most basic needs. Gender awareness starts about the age of two, and boys' essential needs are the same as everyone else's. Some people consider boys who show they have these basic needs to be 'soft' like girls, and wean boys off needing something from others in case this undermines their capacity to be strong, independent and male.

Yet boys do need. On top of being fed and clothed, all boys need emotional sustenance: to be loved, cherished, appreciated, valued, noticed, admired, understood and accepted. When his needs are left unmet, a boy feels ignored and separate. He may conclude that there's something wrong with him and lose self-esteem. A boy who gets into drugs, crime or violence is possibly reacting, angrily and resentfully, against adults who stopped recognising and meeting his needs before he was ready to become emotionally self-sufficient (if any of us ever are).

1 Boys need love too

Boys will often seek love from parents and other adults close to them in roundabout ways. When they are old enough to make sense of what it means to be male, they may decide this means feeling love but not being soft enough to show it or want it.

It can be hard for a boy to accept that being bouncy and boisterous, and sometimes difficult and destructive, sits comfortably with also needing to lose oneself in the warmth and safety of a cuddle. This may be even harder for older boys, particularly if the arms are female. So boys will often use more aggressive tactics to get the love they need than girls, who have far less emotional distance to travel to claim their emotional birthright.

If he's just jumped on you from behind or given you a painful punch, this can mean that he needs your love, so it is better to respond affectionately than to lash out because you feel 'got at'. The aim should be to reduce the parental ties gradually without leaving him feeling emotionally stranded and abandoned.

Parents

- beware of thinking, 'I didn't get or need demonstrations of love, so he'll be the same'; he is different, and those who don't get can turn this into 'don't need' to hide sadness

- if you feel strange giving him cuddles, ask before and after if it is all right for you to do so

- blow kisses if kissing him feels intrusive

- love can also be shown by sitting close while watching TV or reading, for example, or sitting on his bed at night

- you can show love by being interested in his ideas, paying attention to and doing things with him and understanding his feelings

Teachers

- teachers will not feel parental love for the boys in their class; however, they can make it clear that they enjoy, approve of and accept the charges for whom they are responsible

- giving special tasks to certain boys who lack confidence can make them feel significant, noticed, reliable and trustworthy

2 Show that you understand him

He came home from school one day more bad-tempered than I'd seen for ages. He was rude and offhand. He used words that sounded like playground talk; then I realised he was probably repeating what had been said to him. He flung his arms round me and cried with relief that I had understood.

All children find being misunderstood hugely frustrating. It starts as an irritation, but when the mistake persists, a boy will begin to question whether his version of himself is normal, reasonable and justified. When boys consider their wishes are continuously ignored or misinterpreted, they feel not only humiliated but also increasingly resentful, angry and, more damagingly, self-doubting.

Understanding can be shown through anticipating his needs and – carefully – expressing his possible thoughts. You can say things like: 'I guess you're feeling a bit left out. Am I right?' This gives him room to disagree, and stops you coming across as infuriatingly all-knowing – and possibly wrong.

Parents

- accept how he sees the world; he doesn't have to agree with you, nor you with him

- value his uniqueness; tell him what you like about him

- look behind his behaviour for possible causes and feelings; let him know that you know

- repeat what he says to you, to check you've understood: 'So you want me to stay in tonight because you're fed up with me working late so much this week, is that right?'

- remember his likes/dislikes

- state what he's likely to feel about something: 'You're not going to like this, but I don't want you staying out all night'

Teachers

- make a conscious effort to notice patterns in a boy's work that enable you to see him as an individual: 'You really like painting birds, don't you?' or 'You're always writing about fishing; it must be your passion!'

- encourage class work that shows boys' likes and dislikes, and try to remember a few

- for particularly trying boys, list four reasons why this might be so (excluding 'difficult personality')

- use 'reflective-listening' phrases: 'what I hear you saying is that you did not feel you knew enough to begin this homework. Let's start from what you're sure you know'

3 Approve of who he is, even if you hate what he does

Every boy needs to be accepted and approved for who he is, not just because he has been 'good' or 'successful' and lived up to your ideal of who he should be. If he constantly tries to fill a mould fashioned by you, he'll quickly lose his shape and identity and find it hard to be sure about who he is.

Young boys probably get told off more than girls. They are often more boisterous and noisy; they are more prone to accidents, because they're less well co-ordinated; and less able to explain themselves, because their language develops later. Clumsy reprimands convey disapproval and can do great damage. If you have to tell him off for these things, separate the person from his actions. This will leave his self-worth intact while he learns to manage his behaviour and understand its consequences.

A boisterous boy is often fit and fun as well as tiring. Don't lose faith in him just because you are unhappy about a particular act or attitude. Don't ever make him feel devastated by your criticism.

Parents

* think about his good points before you comment on his behaviour, to help you think positively

* avoid using the words 'good' or 'bad' about your son's behaviour, because he'll take them as reflections of himself; instead, describe what it is you approve or disapprove of

* saying: 'Right now, I find your behaviour...' also limits your disapproval to the moment

* hitting him with your hand or an object will make him feel you dislike him

Teachers

* identify something you like in each student, then it's easier to say with honesty that it's his behaviour that's the problem, not the boy himself

* describe in detail the behaviour that is outside the rules and avoid 'You' statements; saying 'I'm finding the way you are tapping your ruler irritating' is less personally offensive and provocative than 'You are being really irritating!'

4 Give plenty of praise

Children love to be praised. It is one of the joys of living and working with them to see them beam with pride and pleasure when they do something well and we notice. Children love to please those they care about.

Praise thrills boys because they need it, but it also teaches them self-discipline. Through praise and encouragement, boys get clear, positive messages about how they should lead their lives – what it is they should do – instead of only hearing about what it is they should not be doing.

Many people, especially men, find it hard to give praise, particularly to boys. Criticising and blaming make them feel in charge and all-knowing. Praising, on the other hand, can make them believe they've lost that powerful edge, which feels dangerous. Some don't know what to praise or what words to use. Others believe praise will make a boy big-headed, or lazy and over-satisfied with work that isn't perfect. But being noticed and appreciated usually makes boys try harder, and it teaches them to appreciate others too.

Parents

* to show approval, we can say: 'That's great!', 'Brilliant', and 'Well done!' 'Thanks, that was really helpful' shows appreciation

* find something to praise, appreciate and notice every day

* boys can be praised for their thinking skills (e.g., choices, ideas, ability to solve problems), social skills (e.g., helpfulness, understanding, sharing and resolving conflicts) and physical skills (e.g., being good with scissors, making things, sport), as well as for good work

* be specific: praise what your son has done rather than go on about how wonderful he is

* praise the effort he's made more than the end product

Teachers

* encourage boys to judge their own work, not to rely on your view

* let them evaluate each other's work, so that praise doesn't always come from people in authority

* help them to feel proud of good work. Assume a boy is proud and say: 'I expect you felt pleased with this piece of work when you finished it'

* find something about them to praise every day, including their humour, sociability and creativity

* for a boy who rejects all praise, showering him with it won't work; select one thing you truly find pleasing, and mention it three times every day for three weeks, so that he begins to believe and trust it is true

5 Spend time with him

I know my dad loves me, but I hardly know him. I know he works hard to support us, but we hardly ever talk. It makes me feel as if I am incomplete.

Survey after survey shows that children like to have their parents around, even if they're not actively doing anything with them. They like to see their fathers as much as their mothers, and boys need their parents' time as much as girls. Even teenage boys want to see more of their parents.

In Britain, men work longer hours than in most other European countries. This means that they spend less time at home with their families. Boys cannot feel loved and lovable, believed in and believable, respected and respectable, if the people on whom they depend seem not to care. Only if the important adults in a boy's life give him time and attention can he feel validated and develop any kind of self-worth. Meeting his need for stress-free time with you, when you focus solely on him, will help him to feel confident and successful.

Parents

• presents are no substitute for presence: don't try to buy your way out of being with your son

• when you're with him, put the answerphone on and spend time finding out what he thinks, and talk about what he has been doing and playing

• play with him, join in or watch him doing his favourite activity, or say: 'I'd love you to talk to me while I wash the car'

• keep every promise you make to visit, and stay in regular touch

• quiet time together can be as valuable as action-packed time

• try to do any work you need to do at home so you're not cut off from your family

Teachers

• boys often play up to get attention.; don't let bad behaviour be the only way they succeed in getting it

• if a boy wants a conversation at an inconvenient moment, suggest another time when you can give him your undivided attention

• identify the quiet boys each week, and organise with colleagues to make a special effort to speak to and engage daily with them in some way

6 Talk with touch and words

Touch can reassure as well as relax. A boy who is never touched can feel ignored, ashamed and unworthy. His confusion about his need for the affirmation that is conveyed through affectionate touch may make him less confident about touching others as an adult, either with formal handshakes or in physical shows of affection with his own children and partners.

Touch can communicate better than words. It can say so much, in so many ways, and it is less open to misinterpretation. And it need only take a split second. The positive touch can be a full embrace or an arm round your son's shoulders; it can ask for nothing in return or seek a simple sign from him that he has acknowledged your gesture. It can demonstrate to him and to others that he belongs to you. It can heal an argument and say you're sorry. It can console him after a disappointment, show how proud you are, or express equality and partnership. But touch can also hurt. Hitting is hurtful, and merely pushing your son away when you're angry can signal deep rejection.

Parents

* little strokes of his forehead, head or hands at bedtime or while watching TV – or just sitting close – can be a way to introduce touch into your relationship

* experiment with little touches to replace words

* if your son finds being touched difficult or embarrassing, ask him what's OK and when

* consider buying him a pet to help him feel comfortable about expressing affection through touch

* ask your partner to massage, stroke or hug you as a reminder of how good it feels; this may make it easier for you to be more expressive with your son

Teachers

* child-protection issues make many teachers reluctant to touch children; in any case, as boys grow older, it becomes increasingly difficult and inappropriate to do so; just standing close to a boy while looking over his work can show you accept him and feel no discomfort in his presence

* some teachers greet their class of young children individually as they enter the classroom, inviting each boy to choose how he wishes to say hello each time – with a smile, a handshake, or nothing at all if that's how he feels that day

7 Respect his right to know

Boys in particular like to live within rules and structure. They thrive when they feel secure and can predict what is going to happen to them. The unexpected can be very unsettling. Sometimes things happen out of the blue and any adults involved can be equally surprised. But more often the adults know in advance and simply fail to keep a child properly informed.

Children need to be able to make sense of their world. If they can't, they live in social and emotional chaos. They make sense of their life both through the patterns that emerge when life is ordered and each day has a predictable shape to it; and through being given explanations when there are changes. Young children's brains develop through constructing meaningful patterns, so every child needs to make sense of knowledge and events before he can learn.

When you explain things to your son, you show that you respect his right to know, empathise with his need to make sense of his world, respect his ability to comprehend and understand, and trust him with the information.

Parents

* try to tell your son about things before they happen, as they happen, and afterwards explain why something happened

* you can tell him about your own feelings and discuss his

* he can be told about changes in routines, partners and relationships and about absences

* he can be told about your decisions, and the reasons for them

* you can give him facts, answering his questions about such things as death and divorce honestly, but in terms which he can comfortably comprehend

Teachers

* give boys good warning of any changes to the daily routine of the classroom

* if you know that you're going to be away, tell them in advance, and let them know who'll be taking your place

* explain why any punishment or 'consequence' is being imposed

* explain fully why a piece of work is either good or falls short of the required standard

* keep boys informed about the time it will take to mark important tests or projects, and explain any delay in returning work to them

8 Boys do best when an involved man cares

Boys do well in all types of families, but they are more secure when a caring man is involved. This man may be a father, relative, neighbour, youth leader or someone from his school. We know from studies that the earlier this special relationship can be established, the better; but otherwise the maxim 'Better late then never' certainly applies.

Boys benefit from a special relationship with a father figure for three reasons: first, being with someone who obviously enjoys his company and is interested in what he does will give him faith in himself; second, having a good relationship with a male 'mentor' and positive role model will show him what he can become; third, the personal qualities of this person will enhance his understanding of people and extend his choices about how to behave.

Fathers can't always be this person, for various reasons. Try not to let jealousy stop somebody else you know from getting close to your son. Provided the relationship is a positive one, and you are sure there's nothing wrong going on, boys benefit from a reliable man giving them his full attention.

Parents

● a relationship with a father figure may start naturally, but if it doesn't, you could start by inviting a possible 'mentor' on an outing with you, or invite him round for tea or to watch a video with you and your son

● identify your son's interests, and ask neighbours if they have similar likes or hobbies and could support your son with his

● don't put your son off someone who is showing an interest, or say hurtful things like 'Why does he think you're so special?' You may think your son is a trial, but this won't be everyone's view

Teachers

● research shows that boys have been turned away from a life of crime or drugs by a teacher who showed a special interest in them and accepted them for who they were; often the teacher was oblivious to his influence

● be aware of any individual's vulnerability and his need to be listened to and understood

● invite suitable men to participate in a range of appropriate class and school-based activities, bearing in mind that police checks now need to be made

● explore the potential of local mentoring with vulnerable boys

9 Be his last point of refuge

When life has been hard for your son, when he has had enough and no longer has the energy to be brave or keep up a front, he'll need somewhere to hide, somewhere and someone to be his last point of refuge. This is the place where he can be himself, and where – for a short time at least – no one is holding him accountable. Here he will feel accepted, unconditionally. This is where he can truly relax, safe in the knowledge that someone is there for him who will take away his burdens when he can no longer carry them.

Home, for children, is the obvious place, and parents are the obvious people, because it is parents who matter most to a child. However, there are times and situations when parents feel they don't have the emotional reserves to give their child the consolation he requires. When this happens, ask yourself whether your son wants any more than for you to be close to him, without saying or doing anything else. This may be all he needs.

Parents

• if he asks for forgiveness after a difficult incident, accept his olive branch and try to put the whole thing behind you

• giving him refuge does not mean you have to ignore forever behaviour that you have found difficult

• take the waiting out of wanting; anticipate his feelings and volunteer solace when you can see that he needs it

Teachers

• boys can find it especially hard to admit errors and may get themselves into further trouble by offering multiple and increasingly thin excuses; try to intervene and forgive before he digs himself in too deep

• some boys rely on school for their solace, so make sure it's on offer somewhere

• help boys to be aware of this need through class discussion of who they may go to and when, where and why

• peer counselling or befrienders' schemes can make boys more willing to seek refuge within school

10 Make him feel he belongs

Human beings have a profound need to feel they belong somewhere and to someone. Your son's first need will be to feel loved by the two people who made him, but as he grows up, the more friends, groups and institutions he feels a bond with and can identify with, the deeper will be his sense of self. Fitting in somewhere says something about who he is and reassures him that there are others like him. Belonging to a family, a social or ethnic group, a club or school, or a place of worship, also means that he is wanted, accepted and acceptable. It provides him with guidelines about who he is and how he should behave.

If a boy grows up without any sense of belonging to his family or school, if he feels rejected – for example, because of heavy criticism – he is likely to seek acceptance and a sense of membership elsewhere. He will seek groups of boys who have opted out of trying to please, and gain pleasure and status in unacceptable ways.

Parents

• tell him family stories, so that he knows his and your roots

• include him in as many family events as possible

• understand how fashion and uniforms can be symbols of belonging, and help him to 'fit in' – provided it fits in with your family budget

• let him attend big school events such as fetes and concerts so that he feels he belongs there

• be on the look-out for signs of 'aloneness'; suggest that he join a sports or social club or youth group if he spends a lot of time alone

Teachers

• circle time and similar arrangements can reinforce group identity and make each child feel an equal member of the class

• stable groups allow a clear identity to form; staff and student changes and regroupings should be minimised for boys who may be especially vulnerable

• where there is a high turnover of students throughout the year (known as 'turbulence'), constant efforts will be required to re-establish the coherence of the class group

11 Allow him some privacy

My mother wanted to know everything about me, especially how I thought about things. It drove me mad and I felt sort of invaded. One day I screamed, 'Stop trying to get inside my head!'

Having time and space just for yourself is part of growing up and becoming separate and independent. Growing boys need this, and parents should not get upset when their son tries to carve out territory that belongs exclusively to him or from which they are totally excluded. This territory might involve his body; it might be his bedroom; it might be his social life; it will very likely be his sex life. If he chooses to look at magazines in the privacy of his bedroom and you find out, it should not be broadcast to family or friends.

Younger boys who feel the need for privacy may try to keep school and parents apart. It won't necessarily be because they have something to hide, just that they need some space.

Parents

• if school becomes his private space, try to give him more privacy elsewhere – in his head or in his room – so that he lets you in

• respect his need for some aspects of his life to belong to him alone; don't feel it's a personal campaign against you

• some children who feel 'invaded' or controlled by their parents will create a private world of their own that involves a great deal of fantasy, to the point of habitually lying

Teachers

• school is a very crowded and public place in which both action and participation are valued highly; boys whose home space is confined and similarly crowded may need to seek their privacy within school

• quiet rooms, or corners in classrooms, may help to meet this need

• boys who don't participate in certain lessons may be taking private time

• a boy's need for some time and space on his own should be respected

12 Encourage a caring masculinity

Boys will be able to feel more at one with themselves and at ease with one another if they can develop their caring instincts in parallel with other features of their personality. Masculinity does not have to be identified solely with physicality, aggression, brutality, crudity or cruelty, to the exclusion of other, softer characteristics.

No one is suggesting that boys lose their gender identity to become like girls or that men ignore the effects of their hormones to ape women. We all, women included, have a tough side and a tender side. Boys' self-esteem will rise when they don't have to deny important bits of themselves.

A recent survey estimated that five million workers are bullied each year, which represents a lot of misery. Of course, women can bully too, but it is likely that more people in a position to bully will be men. When we fail to challenge young children's view of masculinity as associated only with power, aggression and control, the damage to individuals can be widespread.

Parents

• give him permission to feel and express tenderness towards cuddly toys, babies, animals and his younger brothers and sisters

• teach him to care for other people

• try not to belittle any men you know or hear about who take on caring jobs or roles

• don't tolerate hurtful talk or behaviour simply because you think 'boys will be boys'

Teachers

• encourage a policy of zero-tolerance across all classrooms of macho talk that is based on violence, aggression or insensitivity

• avoid timetabling community service as an alternative to sport; playing sport is not incompatible with spending time with elderly people

• ensure plenty of class discussion to raise awareness of caring and gender issues

13 Support him when he's stressed

Contrary to common belief, stress is not something suffered only by adults. In fact, children get a double dose, from events in their own lives, such as bullying, academic pressure and friendship problems, and from the knock-on effect of adult stress, because we all behave less skilfully towards children when we're preoccupied by our own problems. Add to this the fear that a boy will have less experience of life and himself to trust that 'normality' will resume, and we can see that he is likely to get more confused and disorientated than adults, not less.

Stressful events that can destabilise a boy are those that involve separations from those close to him, and changes to his status and self-image or to the pattern of his life, in either routines or relationships.

Signs that he may be feeling distressed about something include a prolonged sad and unhappy mood, becoming withdrawn, disturbed sleep, being very tired, being unusually thirsty, tummy and other pains, aggression, stealing, poor concentration and inattention, and becoming more clingy.

Parents

• spend more time with him, help to boost his self-esteem and ensure he gets plenty of sleep

• take his worries and his view of what he'd like to happen seriously

• keep him informed of changes and decisions, so he feels more in control, and maintain regular routines to bolster his security

• giving emotional support to needy boys is tiring; get more rest so you feel more able to give

Teachers

• brief yourself about and watch out for all the possible signs of distress in your students, including poor work, bad behaviour, visits to the school nurse and truancy, and respond accordingly

• try to find some time to talk to any boy who seems withdrawn and tired in class

• talk to colleagues and contact the boy's home if your worries continue

• be aware that your own stress levels may make you less tolerant of challenging behaviour

CHAPTER 3

Deepening His Self-knowledge and Self-awareness

Boys feel very acutely the expectations of their families and society. The ideal man is supposed to be all-coping, all-powerful, all-knowing. To live up to this image, some boys feel they have to put up a front and deny not knowing all the answers, ignoring their natural sensitivity and instinctive aversion to wrongdoing. The more they follow this path, whether to protect themselves from ridicule or their parents from disappointment, the more boys cut themselves off from who they really are. As they do this, they in effect discard parts of themselves and create a dangerous void in which their feelings are so denied that they are unable to reflect on the causes and consequences of their actions.

The denial process can start early. How many parents, particularly fathers, feel comfortable with their young son wanting a light on at night, a dummy beyond babyhood, or someone to stay with him while he falls asleep? How many teachers taunt boys for shying away from catching a fast ball, having an inoculation or cutting up an animal in Biology? Boys need courage, but it should grow from inner self-confidence.

Our feelings make us who we are. When we are babies, our perceptions and passions give us our first sense of self. So we must take note of what pleases, frustrates, upsets or hurts us.

Knowing our feelings about things has practical relevance, too, for motivation and progress. In order to develop, boys have to know what they are capable of and what they need to learn before they can master a skill. Our ability to look inside ourselves enables us to have a sense of awe and wonder, and to appreciate beauty and understand others. Lasting intimate relationships depend on it.

Research shows that boys find it hard to evaluate themselves. Not only do they avoid doing it, they are frequently over-confident so fail to do enough preparation for exams and under-perform. When they fail, they explain it away by saying that everything will be fine if they try harder. Boys tend to cling to their inflated sense of self, which means any deficit cannot be admitted, let alone tolerated. Parents don't help their sons if they demand flawless children.

Self-awareness promotes emotional literacy, i.e., the capacity to notice and respect other people's sensitivities. We understand others through understanding ourselves. Those who live and work with boys have a duty to help them develop their sense of self by stimulating self-knowledge.

14 Offer choices

Choice is all around us. It's great, because it gives us more control over our lives. Common sense tells us that children should also have choices, but how much, when and, just as important, why?

In a world of multiple choices, boys need to be able to make informed and responsible decisions. Your son will do this better if he understands his own preferences, is sure enough about them to resist outside pressure, and can think through the consequences of his choices upon himself and others. These thinking and reflective skills should be developed wherever possible.

Choice is important because it offers scope for self-determination. It enables a boy to feel he has some control over his life and that he is not powerless and put upon: docility is not a useful quality for the future. Choice also helps to sharpen his sense of himself because it makes him consider what he really wants.

Parents

• younger children can be given some choice about what or how much they want to eat or drink, what they wear, what they play, who they play with and what story they have at bedtime

• avoid suggesting that they go out and play with someone; allow them to come up with ideas and playmates for themselves

• older boys can have some choice about, e.g., when and where they do their homework, what (but not how much) TV they watch, what they spend their pocket money on, and so on

Teachers

• respect a student's decisions – don't ask him what he wants, then ignore his reply

• choices help to manage behaviour in the classroom; say: 'You can carry on talking and mucking about, or you can get a detention. It's your choice'

15 Manage choices

In larger families, meeting everyone's whims and wishes is usually impossible. It isn't good for children, or for parents, either. Too much choice can undermine a boy's sense of self: if he never makes true choices, he won't discover what he really likes best. He can also become confused and unhappy if he has too many choices about too many things, because he won't feel that his parents are in charge and family rules will be blurred.

Too much choice can easily lead to arguments, since he won't realise when his demands go too far. In addition, it allows him to control and manipulate situations; it doesn't prepare him to cope with disappointment; it may encourage him to become selfish and insensitive to other people's needs; and it can take responsibility from him because he can always say, 'Sorry, wrong choice – I'll have this one,' if he doesn't like the consequences of his initial decision.

To help a boy strengthen and deepen his self-esteem, the choices offered must be both limited and managed.

Parents

• managed choice means 'either/or' decisions; you put limits on the choices, having already decided what you are happy to agree to

• limited choice means offering these choices only a few times a day

• avoid open-ended choices; for example, on a cold day, it's better to say: 'Would you like to wear your jeans or your tracksuit today?' in case he chooses shorts, and no more than three items should be on the breakfast menu

• make sure the choices you offer are realistic

• boys should not normally be in charge of how the whole family spends its time

Teachers

• choice is motivating; boys who are given some choice about what they do and how they do it are often more committed to their work

• offer choice within project work – not too much or it becomes too hard to start, but enough to foster individuality

• where there is little scope for choice in lesson work, choice-based activities can be tried, such as 'If I could be a tree/food/colour/musical instrument/car/country/piece of furniture/an animal, I'd be a ..., because ...'

16 Don't impose your views on him

My father was insufferable. He couldn't discuss anything; he just stated his view and declared all others to be uninformed and stupid. He tried to tell me what to think and how to do everything. When I needed to survive on my own, I found it hard to get his voice out my head.

It's very easy to become so convinced by your own status and wisdom as a parent or adult that you assert your own opinions, issue unilateral declarations, and impose your own decisions almost without realising it, squashing your son's growing need to discover where he stands.

Too much criticism or praise, or the extensive use of rewards, can have the same result: you are asking your son to live exclusively by your views and values, giving no space for his own to take shape. There has to be a balance. Children, particularly during adolescence when they deconstruct themselves before they reconstruct, often explore their new identity by rejecting any parental model. They should be free to cross that road without being run over.

Parents

* seek his views; say things like: 'I like it, but it's what you think that's important' not 'That's great, don't you think?' or 'What did you make of that TV programme?' not 'That was a load of rubbish'

* think carefully about the things you care about, and realise he is likely to target those as he breaks away; if he does, don't take it personally

* with older boys, the more you push your views and values and assume they should share them, the more likely they are to reject them

Teachers

* encourage students to think ahead about what might happen next in, for example, a science experiment, rather than telling them what they should expect

* resist the temptation to deliver the standard arguments for and against something in classwork in order to save time; ask your students for their views

* if you get involved in sorting out a conflict between two boys, don't impose solutions on them but encourage them to come up with their own

* in general debates, however strongly you feel about an issue, keep your views to yourself and allow boys to explore theirs; this does not mean you cannot question and gently challenge

17 Give his feelings space in your world

As a lad, I was forced to live on an emotional plateau – never allowed to express unbound joy or the depths of sadness. Being constrained by moderation in all things suffocated me and I almost lost myself. My own son jumps up and down when he's happy, and I love to see it.

How many times have people said to you, 'You've no right to feel that'? Didn't it make you boil, and feel small? Times have, hopefully, moved on. We now understand that feelings are as important as thoughts in the development of our children as unique and giving human beings. If we reject our son's feelings, we reject him as he experiences himself.

Feelings used to be thought of as somehow inferior to thoughts, more closely associated with instinct and animals, something that governed human beings when we were primitive, not civilised and sophisticated. But feelings are often a rational response to a situation, and can be crucial to survival.

Parents

• if you accept his feelings, he will learn to live with, manage and enjoy them also

• teach your son to ask for what he needs; 'I think you're feeling upset. Would a hug help?' can free him to say, 'I'm feeling upset so I've come for a hug'

• accept his apologies, and you can say, 'I snapped at you because I was fed up about something that happened today. I'm sorry.'

• it's fine to feel, but not to hurt; jealousy, anger, frustration and resentment have to be managed, not buried

• older boys often use music to explore/express feelings

Teachers

• give boys incomplete sentences to fill in, such as: 'I'm happiest when ...', 'When I get angry, I...', 'I feel most important when...', 'I feel frustrated when...', 'I tend to give up when...', etc.

• brainstorm *anger*; invite your class to discuss how they feel/see *anger*; suggest similes for it, such as powerlessness, rage, frustration, etc.; ask students to describe relevant situations, and to consider whether the feeling described fits any labels being discussed

• have each child write in a 'feelings' log book at set (and free) times about their reactions to pieces of work, school or events

18 Tell him his story

You took your first steps running away from the vacuum cleaner. It used to terrify you. One day, when it came close, you just took off!

Young boys love to be told stories about themselves – when they were babies, how any older brothers and sisters reacted when they arrived, and so on. These stories give your son a history. They are pieces of his life's jigsaw that he needs to complete his picture.

Older children like to hear other stories – about your childhood and school days, or the antics of their aunts and uncles. Such tales deepen your son's sense of belonging, as he learns more about what it is he belongs to. Each story will act as a connecting thread that will create a sense of continuity in him. Like a spider's web, the more linking threads there are, the stronger he will feel.

Difficult times need to be talked about too. If you blank them out, it will not only break the thread and leave a gap in his history but also damage his confidence about the future.

Parent

• get out family photos from time to time; talk about the people and events shown in them; this can fill in gaps in his understanding of family history, generate laughter, lead to further conversations, reinforce your son's identity and increase his confidence

• regularly recall past holidays, birthdays or treats that were fun and brought the family together

• if you can, collect and keep for your son items such as favourite toys, books, clothes and first shoes, so that he may revisit the past and bring it to life

• talk about difficulties; don't bury them; he has a right to information about himself

Teachers

• personal life-lines: in a group, discuss special experiences that have marked students' lives, and what made them significant, how they felt at the time, etc.; ask each child to draw a vertical line on a large sheet of paper (the line represents their life from birth to the present) and to write their own personal positive and negative events on either side of the line

• not everyone has a happy family story to tell; focus on good and bad, happy and sad experiences, to ensure a full and realistic picture that leaves no one out

19 Encourage reflection

Reflection means standing outside oneself, looking in at what has happened and asking questions like why, how and what if? It means 'to consult with oneself' and 'to go back in thought'. Reflection entails reliving your experiences and having a silent conversation with yourself to understand them and the connections between them. You get to know and understand yourself better through reflection. It helps you make sense of your life; but it is something that many boys find difficult.

It is a good idea to encourage boys to reflect, because thinking backwards is the first step to thinking forwards, which is important for learning, keeping relationships, managing conflict without violence and planning one's life. If boys cannot reflect on their views and actions, assess the good and the bad and work out what they might need to change, they will be unable to develop or make progress in anything. Becoming aware of how they feel and behave helps them to understand other people's feelings and behaviour and, therefore, to anticipate any problems with others. Understanding their past helps them to face the future.

Parents

* recap and reflect on the day's events with your son each night as part of his bedtime routine, and invite him to 'think aloud' about both good and bad aspects of it

* do it yourself; saying things like: 'I wonder if I could have done that another way?' and 'I really felt excited/angry (etc.) when it happened', or apologising show reflection in action

* read books with story lines to your son from as early an age as possible

* encourage imaginative play and dressing up

Teachers

* ensure that boys read fiction regularly as well as non-fiction, and discuss story lines and characters

* encourage lots of discussions about 'what if' situations

* introduce role reversal in drama to explore alternative experiences

* ask boys to write down two negative and two positive descriptions of themselves on two pieces of paper; transfer them to a large board and ask: 'Are you always irritating? When? Why?' and so on, to help them see their behaviour is connected with specific situations

20 Arrange wind-down and quiet time

The typical boy is a bundle of energy who needs to be on the go and to let off steam, but he also needs to be able to slow down when the situation or a person requires it and to feel comfortable within himself when he does stop. Activity is great, but children are more likely to explore their inner selves when they are quiet.

Quiet time means the chance to be calm, to wind down, relax or even escape. Quiet time also means peaceful togetherness, being at rest and content to be alone. Each boy has his own way of unwinding. One will prefer to flop in front of the television; another will require the boundaries of a bath to contain him. Some choose to relax by kicking a ball, others will be happy to contemplate and reflect as they draw or doodle.

Being quiet at such times gives a boy the chance to let his thoughts roam, to find out what is inside him and learn to be at peace with and within himself.

Parents

- discover his mechanisms for winding down – especially after rough-and-tumble play and after school, when he can find it hard to 'come down' – and encourage him to do it

- respect his need for his own quiet space, even if it is not in your home

- encourage quiet togetherness – watch TV or a video together, make time for morning cuddles in bed if he is still young, or drive him to his friends' houses sometimes

Teachers

- simple breathing and relaxation exercises can work very well with primary school children; older boys may need considerable encouragement to participate, but it's worth a try

- have a clear ending planned for lessons, especially those in which there has been a lot of activity; use this time to recap, and encourage students to reflect on what has been taught and learned

21 Explain your thoughts and feelings

'Children need models more than they need critics' – so said the French philosopher, Joubert. Boys will learn to identify and express their thoughts and feelings safely and comfortably if they see you do the same.

It is particularly important for boys to see their fathers or male role models being open about their emotions and giving serious thought to their ideas. One significant and unhelpful element of 'macho' maleness is that opinions are asserted in a commanding and dictatorial fashion and presented as 'the truth'. This obliterates the possibility that others, including children, may see things differently.

Thoughts and arguments should be put forward and explained, not asserted, with the possible exception of key matters of discipline. A useful principle is: assert your right to be heard, not your view of the world. Inner strength is based on tolerance and respect, not domination, and such a view is also hugely liberating: if you don't need to dominate, you don't always need to be right.

Parents

• if you are angry, upset or frustrated, explain why; don't just shout

• when you explain your reactions to your son's actions, he learns to assess and anticipate the results of his behaviour; this helps him to become responsible

• tell him how you arrive at decisions, by saying, e.g.: 'I first thought this, then I realised that, so I decided...'

• you are responsible for your feelings; say: 'I felt angry when...', not 'You made me angry'

• if your son swears, ask him to find an alternative word to express what he's trying to say, and do the same yourself

Teachers

• help your students find the best language with which to express their thoughts and feelings

• try always to express yourself as well as possible, too

• use 'I' phrases in order to avoid blaming any individual student or group of students for anything

• emotional literacy requires an emotional vocabulary; boys need to discover which words they can use to express their feelings – and, if information is presented properly to them, will enjoy widening their vocabularies to replace expletives

22 Ensure communication

I thought my son was fine. He seemed to get on with his life, though he was alone a lot, and I got on with mine. We didn't talk much. Then in the middle of his mock A-level exams he crashed. Now he won't work, go out or talk. We're in a real mess.

If children and adults don't communicate, there can be a very high price to pay. Communication skills lie at the heart of social and emotional health and success, and a boy will not be as comfortable with talking if adults, especially parents, don't talk to him. No conversation implies no interest, which he is likely to interpret as neglect, so family silence can have a devastating impact on his self-esteem and his trust in future relationships.

But family conversation also helps a boy to be comfortable about expressing his views to other adults in positions of authority as well as among his own peers. It contributes to confidence and will help him to stand his ground when dealing with professionals and officialdom in the future.

Parents

* keep talking, even if it feels uncomfortable; the more you do it, the easier it will become

* try to eat together as often as possible; if it's only occasional, ignore his bad table manners and swallow hard if he challenges you about controversial subjects

* if you want to take issue with something, start with the word 'I', by saying, e.g., 'I'm not happy with doing all the chores and I'd like some help'

* always stop and listen

* if you have to be away, for work or for pleasure, set aside time on your return to touch base with him again

Teachers

* never assume that withdrawn, silent students are fine, though they make your work as a teacher easier

* although quiet students may simply be taking time out, be alert to longer-term patterns; talk informally and socially to such students, talk to colleagues about them, and step in sooner rather than later when necessary

* vary lesson plans and allow for small-group work, as this encourages involvement and participation

* in all lessons, nurture the skills of communication: reflection, listening and tolerance

23 Encourage self-assessment

Although our children love to know they have pleased us, what we should try to encourage from the start is the confidence to evaluate and praise themselves.

Boys seem to find it particularly hard to self-criticise, and when they do many are too cocky and give themselves more credit than is due. While this confidence can be a delight to see, it can be dangerous, leading to self-satisfaction, laziness, poor preparation and unreal expectations – not to mention wounded self-esteem. Being a boy, facing the demands that he does, your son is just as likely to respond to a shattered ego with denial and pretence as with a resolve to make good the deficit.

Self-assessment is important because it is central to independent learning, which is the way of the future. Many boys find it uncomfortable because they dislike both the responsibility it places on them and admitting that they could have done better. But more experience of self-evaluation is the only way out of this difficulty. The sting is removed from criticism when it comes from themselves.

Parents

• avoid doing all the judging so that your son won't become dependent on your opinion and lose faith in his own

• when your son asks you what you think of something he has done – a painting, an essay, a sports achievement, a music practice – turn the question back to him; what matters, ultimately, is what he thinks of his effort, and getting him used to deciding for himself is crucial

Teachers

• boys can be encouraged to assess each other's work, in pairs, as a first step to becoming honest about their own work

• boys in nursery and infant school work well with 'plan, do, then review', and older boys can do this too

• at the end of any piece of work, boys can be required to say what mark they think it merits, then you can explain why and how it did, or did not, meet the standards for that assessment

• once self-assessment becomes frequent and normal, there will be no excuse for boys being dangerously over-optimistic about their abilities

24 Hear the sound of silence

During adolescence, our son became almost mute. He spent hours in his room and hardly spoke. I was frantic, but it was the same for a few of my friends, so gradually I relaxed about it. He got through it, of course, and since he started college, he's back to his old self.

This parent eventually trusted his instinct and things turned out okay, but take care. If your son withdraws and becomes more silent, you cannot necessarily assume that everything is normal, because it might not be. His behaviour could be a sign of unhappiness and depression.

However, your son does not have to talk all the time. Silence can mean he feels comfortable and does not need to fill every moment with words; it can be understood as quiet togetherness. The important thing is not to ignore it when a boy becomes quiet. Hear the silence, reflect on it, accept it for a time, see if you can find out what he is doing with it. And step in if you believe he is withdrawn from others as well as yourself, and if there are additional signs of problems.

Parents

• keep talking to your son – about things that won't start an argument – but don't force him to respond

• suggest doing something together that doesn't rely on talking but that you can share, like swimming, bowling, or going to a football match

• watch out for signs of difficulty or danger, such as leaving late for or missing school frequently, changes in his eating patterns, unusual smells that could indicate lone drug or alcohol use, and any drop in the standard of his personal care

Teachers

• small-group activities encourage participation and offer less chance to hide behind silence

• a boy who clams up in the classroom may be afraid of making mistakes or be distracted by problems; it's important to find out why he does not talk

• try introducing activities that require every person to speak in turn

CHAPTER 4

Giving Him a Positive View of Himself

To manage the change and uncertainty that will characterise the twenty-first century, boys need to learn to see themselves and their capabilities in a positive light. If your son is to be able to manage several career changes successfully, adapt to new situations and markets, sell himself as a self-employed consultant or skilled craftsman, or negotiate constructively within relationships, he must believe in himself and feel he has many talents to offer. If he grows up seeing himself as a source of pain, distress, disappointment and disaster, he won't have confidence to take on challenges or commitments.

So how can adults help to create boys who are motivated, enthusiastic and full of optimism? It is vital to be supportive, extend their horizons and give them plenty of positive feedback, but it is also essential that we cut down on blame, nagging and criticism; they send harmful messages about how likeable and competent our sons are, with damaging consequences for their emotional stability, self-esteem and motivation.

Not only sticks and stones hurt. We can appreciate that hurtful things said to a boy in the playground will wound him. It is far harder to acknowledge that our own constant criticism will make a boy feel there's something wrong with him and undermine his confidence, independence, initiative and morale. He will be looking over his shoulder all the time, hearing your voice, wondering which of his actions will be next in line for your disapproval. Shouting, unwarranted blame and harsh, erratic punishment have a similar effect; they shatter his security.

We find many ways to justify our negative words and excuse ourselves. We may believe he deserved it or knows we really love him, or see his challenging reactions as a sign that our words didn't hurt, not realising the shield he raises is a protective fiction. Men, especially, may believe a boy needs toughening up if they sense he is easily hurt. But a boy who 'can't take constructive criticism' has, in fact, taken a bucketful of it and should be given no more if he is to have any energy left to protect his self-respect.

Neglect hurts, too. Institutionalised teenage offenders consistently mention feeling neglected by parents who lead lives in which they hardly feature and who allow them too much freedom for their age, which they interpret as indifference. What counts to a boy is not his parent's declaration that he is loved, but whether this has been actively demonstrated to his satisfaction.

25 Understand his particularities

Every boy is different. A boy can be adaptable, affectionate, funny, sensitive, quick to cry, find it hard to concentrate or to share, live in a fantasy world or be down-to-earth. He can be resilient, jealous, generous, prosaic or fanciful, like noise or quiet, be tidy or untidy, seek company or prefer solitude. He may feel, play, think, learn, and enjoy things in a way that is different from other people. It is these 'particularities' which define who he is as a human being, regardless of his gender. A boy will have a clearer picture of the different elements within himself if close adults put what they see into words.

To take the analogy of an artist's palette, the more 'colours' or traits that can be identified, the more varied and interesting the picture that is painted. Parents, and sometimes teachers, often see a boy as 'naughty'. If he is not 'good' (which for those parents means never doing anything wrong), then he is automatically 'naughty'. In that situation, boys learn to see themselves as either good or bad, and if it's the latter, unsuccessful too.

Parents

• fill in your son's 'personality palette'. Write down his likes and dislikes – what he likes to or won't eat, his favourite games, pastimes and activities, clothes, what he does well, places he likes to go, how he works best

• be positive: traits you view as negative may be the reverse side of positive ones; for example, he may stand up for himself with friends but be 'too assertive' with you

• tell him what you see: 'I really like the way you...', or 'You're very sensitive, aren't you?'

Teachers

• consult with other staff members to determine specific strengths and weaknesses of a student you find 'difficult'

• be aware of different learning styles (ask what students prefer) and vary lessons appropriately

• ask students to get into small groups; in each group, select one student and have the rest of the group bombard him with all the strengths and unique features they see in him (no negative comments are allowed); one person should record the contributions, listing ten to fifteen of his strengths

26 Don't compare him to others

For some boys, living in the shadow of a brother or sister is a nightmare that stays with him for the rest of his life. He can never quite shake off the humiliation and feeling of inferiority. Comments like: 'Your brother would not have produced work like that' or 'You're not as talented as your sister' can ruin pride and kill ambition. Friends, too, can be used (or rather abused) as a model for him to measure up to, in questions like: 'Why can't you do as well as Jonathan?' But far from acting as a spur, adults who suffered these taunts as children say their childhood was tainted by them.

Even handing out equal praise can be limiting. Saying: 'Dan's the brainy one in the family and Jim's the athlete' may give each brother something to be proud of, but it will make it less likely that either will explore their potential to do well in the other's field of interest. Brothers and sisters may be genuinely different, but they also make themselves different in order to create their own territory, and when skills become territories, children can become tribal.

Parents

● every child responds – and is entitled to respond – differently to situations because each child is unique;   comparisons will undermine his self-confidence

● make it clear there is room for more than one artist, poet, pianist or tennis player in the family

● labelling causes resentment, and may tempt a boy to do and become the opposite out of pique

● don't compare your son with how you were or what you did at his age; he is himself, not you

Teachers

● positively value each child as an individual – references to siblings should never be used to damn or coerce work

● be especially supportive of originality and creativity

● the most useful comparison, if one is to be made, is self-referential: compare each boy's current performance or piece of work with his last

27 Respect his feelings

Feelings are fundamental; they make us who we are. Many parents find it hard to accept that their boys can be fearful and anxious. Men aren't supposed to have those vulnerabilities, and the sooner a boy overcomes them, the sooner his parents can be reassured that their son is going to be a 'real' man, and also stop having to spend valuable time and energy dealing with those fears and feelings. Fear of the dark, water, spiders, losing friendships, failure, nightmares and bogeymen all seem irrational to parents and test their patience. They respond with rational arguments, but, for the boy, the fear may be purely emotional and, therefore, irrational.

Whether it is delight or disappointment, fear or fury, joy or jealousy, boys are entitled to have their feelings acknowledged and respected by their parents and carers, just as girls are.

Parents

● respect his fears and anxieties

● share his delights and disappointments

● acknowledge and describe how he might be feeling, so that he develops a vocabulary that will help him to understand his reactions

● jealousy is natural, normal and acceptable, but it's not acceptable to hurt anyone because of jealousy

Teachers

● as part of a literacy strategy, junior children can be given a 'feelings' book in which they can write how they felt about particular lessons, projects or homework

● fear of failure explains a wide variety of behaviour that obstructs learning; encourage boys to be open about fears

● at all ages, drama and role-play can allow both boys and girls to explore emotions 'safely'

● debates in mixed gender groups will enable boys to learn more about empathy

● encourage them to explore emotions by reading literature

28 Listen with both eyes

My dad doesn't really listen to me. I'd love him, one day, to put his newspaper down or turn off the TV when I'm talking to him. I feel like a nobody.

Listening involves looking just as much as hearing. When you listen with half an ear, it usually means you are concentrating on something else you are doing, not looking at your son. When you look at him, three things happen: first, you have to stop what you're doing, so that your full attention is available to be directed at him; second, eye contact with him helps you to fix your thoughts on him and what he has to tell you; third, you are able to read his body language and facial expressions, which will help you to interpret any thoughts he may be unable or unwilling to express.

When parents and teachers don't listen properly, or at all, they are conveying the message that they and their business are more important. Boys who are ignored will feel insignificant and undermined, and their self-esteem cannot possibly flourish.

Parents

* when your son wants to tell you something, use your eyes first, not your ears; stop what you're doing and focus on him

* study his facial expression, look for any hidden meaning, notice how he is standing or sitting, and his tone of voice

* let him know you are taking him seriously, and say: 'this sounds important, I think I'd better sit down and listen properly'

Teachers

* show awareness, and say: 'My antennae tell me there is more to this story than you're letting on'

* teach students about body language and be vigilant about its application in all oral activities in the classroom

* provide plenty of opportunity in discussions, debates and presentations for boys to listen to and respect each other's contributions

29 See with both ears

Like listening with both eyes, seeing with both ears means helping adults to be more sensitive to boys and their experiences. A boy's inner world is as important to him as the outer, visible one. Certainly both influence the quality of his self-esteem, but the former is possibly more important.

You get a glimpse of what might be happening inside him from listening to his 'self-talk' – that is, what he says about himself. For example, a boy may seem to be doing fine at school, and have done especially well on a particular test. You then feel you can relax and assume he feels good about himself. He may, however, respond to the result by saying, 'That was a fluke. I didn't deserve it' or 'I'll probably fail next time.' His words show that, inside, he doubts himself. He may have plenty of friends, but if one cries off a visit and he says, 'He's probably had a better invitation,' it again indicates a tendency to put himself down.

Parents

* listen for, and rephrase, negative self-talk

* try to keep a record of what he says and how often he makes such comments, even if in apparent jest, to understand any pattern or the scale of the problem

* simply denying a child's self-criticism won't have much impact; repeat often, over a period of time, that you see him differently; say, e.g.: 'I find you quick to see the point/amusing and fun to be with...' or 'I see you as someone who...'

Teachers

* be positive! Discourage negativity and challenge 'I can't do this' assertions

* encourage self-evaluation tasks in which students write about their performance, highlighting the areas where they believe they performed best

* if a boy says he's no good and knows nothing, draw a horizontal line with 'Knowing nothing' at one end and 'Knowing everything' at the other; invite him to mark the spot that represents how much he really knows, and he'll realise that he does know something

30 Respect his play

As a child, I had a brilliant time, making up stories, getting up to minor mischief, spending hours outside with my friends.

Boys are playful. They love to have fun with both friends and family. Play is essential to the development of self-esteem and confidence. Through play, boys find out who they are, because through the choices they make about what to play or do, who to play with, what to draw, and so on, they gradually flesh out their self-concept and gain an identity, two essential prerequisites for acquiring self-esteem. Through play, boys also discover what they can do, because play develops verbal, social, manual, planning, problem-solving, negotiation and physical skills, which enhance their self-confidence and their ability to socialise and make friends.

Finally, through safely managed, independent play, boys gradually realise that they can manage on their own.

Parents

* encourage your son to play with you, with his friends, on his own, indoors and outdoors

* let him choose what to play most of the time

* respect his play by giving him notice of when he must stop, and by not spoiling his fantasies with teasing or ridicule

* pretending, dressing up, drawing and creative games are just as important for boys as for girls and allow them to become spontaneous, creative and imaginative, all of which help them to do well at school

* get involved in his computer games – it's the way of the future

Teachers

* show respect for students' hobbies and interests; utilise these for individual presentations and projects

* role-play and improvisation can be fun and can provide a great release for boys – giving quiet ones a more assertive role or more ebullient ones a lesser or subservient role

* though play is important, there are times when it is appropriate or must stop; wind-down time after breaks can help to mark boundaries

* respect younger boys' action play, because there is often more of a story line than first appears

31 Let him impress you

Boys get a real boost when someone they admire a great deal shows they are impressed with them. They puff up with extra confidence and pleasure. It does their self-esteem no end of good. Showing you are impressed is, of course, a form of praise, and a very effective and straightforward form of it.

Being impressed has little of the measured judgement implied in some other forms of praise. Most important, it is unconditional. 'I am really impressed!' or 'That was impressive!' says it all – no ifs and buts to qualify or detract from the message. There is nothing grudging about being impressed.

To say you are impressed also clears the air of competition. Some fathers, especially, feel they need to be stronger, better and more clever than their sons – and to prove it. But being impressed doesn't mean a boy has 'won' in some way or will stop trying; it simply shows admiration, which is what boys thirst for.

Parents

• ask him to help you mend things, sort things, decide things, clean things, then say: 'Wow, you're good at that, aren't you? I'm impressed!'

• show you respect his skills and his views; say: 'You're good at mending things – can you help me with this?'

• give him responsibilities so that he can test himself, develop his skills and feel trustworthy; let him know that he has become responsible

• let little ones win in little ways, and show that you're impressed

Teachers

• give boys responsibilities – for example, reporting back from group discussions, looking something up that will benefit everyone's class work – and show how impressed you are with the outcome

• begin questions in the classroom along the lines of: 'Ben, you know quite a lot about this...'

• for an impressive piece of work, gauge the appropriate method of reward, public or private

32 Fight the might of muscles

The classic male body may be the dream of many, but not every boy is going to grow up naturally endowed with broad shoulders and rippling muscles. Many families, and some racial groups, simply don't transmit the right genes to bring this about. Boys may not worry about the pout of their lips, the spread of their buttocks or the size of their eyes, but they experience as much anxiety about body shape and the condition of their skin as pubescent girls.

Muscles take on a special value wherever physical strength is prized above other attributes and where might is viewed as right. If everyone in your family respects social, rather than physical, qualities in human beings, and rejects the use of muscle power to end disputes, your son's self-esteem will flourish, whatever his shape and size. Social and emotional strength matter far more in the long term. It is also important he can freely admit when his body is ill and not working properly.

Parents

• teach him to care for and honour his body, whatever its shape, by supporting him when he's ill and helping him stay clean, fit and healthy

• be careful what you say about men's physique, so you don't applaud media stereotypes

• if he wants to do weight-training, and it's safe, support him, don't tease; but make sure he knows that he's lovable as he is and that girls go for personality and humour more than looks

• don't teach him to hit back at or exploit physical size with other boys

Teachers

• avoid comments such as: 'You're big and strong; you can help me with these books'

• make boys aware of the power of advertising in establishing preferred body images

• talk about what makes a 'real man'

• break down stereotypes through discussion, classroom displays and teaching materials

• initiate work on bullying and operate zero tolerance of physical fights on or near school grounds

33 Lead him when he's ready

My son's just got into Cambridge University. You know, he didn't read properly until he was seven; he just wasn't interested. I wasn't worried then, and now I know I was right.

Parents can't wait for their children to walk, get out of nappies, read, swim, ride a bike and so on, for many different reasons, some more honourable than others, but this eagerness can be counterproductive for a boy's self-esteem.

All children learn best when they are ready. 'Ready' means not only that they're willing – hungry for the knowledge or skill – but also comfortable and confident enough to progress, instinctively aware that the necessary prior knowledge is in place, so they will be able to make sense of what they find.

When a boy can influence what he does and when, he begins to know himself intimately and to trust his judgement, to the long-term benefit of his self-esteem.

Parents

- 'If it's Tuesday, it must be karate.' Some boys are driven, literally and metaphorically, by their parents to attend a stream of after-school activities, to keep them busy and give them opportunities to shine, but children get tired; beware of forcing your son into extra-curricular pursuits which he doesn't enjoy and at which he won't succeed

- avoid pushing him to progress too soon; if you push too hard, he may actually lose ground

Teachers

- encourage 'mastery learning', in which students are told what they are expected to learn, how they are expected to demonstrate their learning, how it will be assessed, and then allowed to choose their own way to meet expectations; such programmes are particularly effective for weaker students

- when a child is motivated, his work improves; try to enhance each boy's motivation so that he may develop as he wishes to

- boys like to learn in and through groups; if a student seems 'stuck', try making him work in a group

34 Accept his friends

We'd all been together through everything, for years. Mum always liked them. When we left school, she paid for us to go out and have a good time together to say thanks to them.

Friends are important to a boy, whatever his age. They make him feel he belongs, that he's liked and likeable. They validate him, share his needs and widen his interests. They help to give him an identity. He thinks: 'I am friends with this sort of person so I am also like this.' Friends help him to fill his time and have fun, to become sociable and learn to be part of a group. They make him more confident and provide the security of safety in numbers.

Real friends will offer support, empathy and loyalty, and be there when things go wrong. His friends will become part of him, which makes it doubly hard if you tell him he's made the wrong choice; reject his friends and you reject him. When his friends 'fit' your family, it gives you a warm feeling of pride and relief that he's accepted by others. It's far harder when children 'get in with the wrong crowd', when friends subvert your plans, challenge your values and cause problems.

Parents

• invite his friends to your home or on outings with you so that you can get to know them better

• tell your son what you like about his friends

• compliment your son on his ability to be a good friend to others

• if his friends are a bad influence, get him to list what he's getting from them and consider whether his needs could be met in another way

• try to talk about what he expects from a real friend – and let him deside whether his 'friends' have these qualities

Teachers

• though natural friendships should be recognised and respected, you should arrange classroom seating and the composition of groups for project work in ways that encourage mixing and minimise peer pressure, bullying and isolation

• explore the issue of friendships and peer pressure through school assemblies, personal and social situations, education and drama

35 Enter his world carefully

My lad became passionate about fishing after he'd been taken a couple of times by his uncle. He desperately wanted me to come too, but it took so long and I had the younger one, so I never did. I told myself I wanted to keep it as his thing and didn't want to muscle in, but when his passion dwindled I realised how badly he'd wanted me to share in his interest. It was my doing that he gave up.

It can be hard to judge the amount of involvement a boy wants us to have in his life, especially when he is at an age when he needs to become more separate and independent. There can be no clear answers – we must simply remain sensitive to the issue and judge each situation as it arises. There are two principles to bear in mind that may be useful: first, show interest, but don't be intrusive, and, second, remember that your prime role is to be his parent rather than his friend. You can be effective and loving without being his best friend, who should come from his peer group.

Parents

- show interest, but don't be intrusive

- share and show an interest in his hobbies but don't take them over; they don't have to become your passion too

- give him the space and territory to be different and separate from you without cutting yourself off

- pop music is frequently used by older boys to explore and establish their new identity; ask which bands they like, but don't make them your favourites

- sporting events can be shared safely, and bring different generations closer

Teachers

- in any class discussions about personal and family matters, acknowledge your students' range of family types and personal experiences, but tread very carefully in these areas

- plan ahead about how you should respond if a student ever becomes distressed during discussions of personal issues

36 Cut down on criticism

Jimmy was ten, and doing well in school, to the delight of his parents. Then he overheard his mum chatting to a friend whose son was struggling. Jimmy's mum didn't want to upset her friend further by parading his success, so she replied, when asked, 'Oh, our Jimmy's no good at anything!' These few words had a devastating effect, destroying his confidence. He never trusted himself again and dropped out of college ten years later. Only then did Jimmy and his mum learn the truth from each other, but it was too late.

Adults are usually totally unaware of the destructive impact of their careless words, which can do untold damage. Even an occasional statement can destroy a future by allowing self-doubt to take root, and boys are as sensitive to criticism as girls. Constant carping and criticism lead to self-doubt and guilt about letting parents down. If a boy fails to please, he'll assume he disappoints; and eventually he'll feel totally useless and rejected, though he will probably hide it well.

Parents

* select one behaviour at a time and ignore the rest; piling on the criticism will make him resentful and uncooperative

* accentuate the positive – say what you want done, and choose a day when you comment only on the good things

* try to stop watching and judging, because this implies you are also controlling and mistrustful

* banish humiliating phrases such as: 'I can't take you anywhere,' 'I wish you'd never been born' and 'You make me sick'

Teachers

* teachers' words can hurt as much as anybody's

* like criticism, teasing, sarcasm, ridicule, shouting and blame are put-downs which hurt, shame, degrade, damage and humiliate; they sap motivation and morale and are never justified

* it takes four 'praises' to undo the harm of one destructive criticism

* turn your don'ts into do's

* doubts are more cruel than the worst of truths – keep a boy's self-doubt at bay

CHAPTER 5

Demonstrating Care Through Love and Rules

One five-year-old boy who had recently started school was asked what he liked best about it. Without hesitation, he replied, 'Assembly, because that's when we get told what we can and can't do.' His mother was very surprised, for he liked to have his own way at home. What she didn't appreciate is how much comfort and security boys find in rules and structure.

One teacher I know believes that boys generally have a more fragile self-esteem than girls, except for those who have grown up with a high degree of consistency at home. These boys knew where they stood and what they could do, were secure enough to learn new things and were happy to take responsibility for themselves.

We show that we care in many different ways. The right kind of food makes him grow strong and healthy. Ensuring that he's clean and appropriately clothed keep him warm and protected from disease and ill health. Having fun and sharing our lives with him make him feel emotionally secure, as does being understanding about the mistakes he will inevitably make as he gains skills, confidence and maturity.

Short cuts don't work. Giving in to a boy because you can't be bothered to argue won't persuade him you care; neither will showering him with presents. Having guidelines for behaviour that will protect him and others demonstrates your concern.

Positive discipline builds positive self-esteem. When there are clear guidelines for behaviour and a daily routine, children can relax. They don't have to decide everything for themselves or worry about getting into trouble and, when they behave, life is not only calmer but filled with the warmth of other people's approval. When adults set limits and are sufficiently involved to monitor a boy's behaviour, he realises that they care.

Of course, rules must be fair and reasonable. The popular phrase 'tough love' does not give adults the right to be brutal. Discipline without dictatorship and punishment without humiliation ensure that boys won't need to challenge perceived unfairness or face parents' put-downs which will eventually shatter their self-esteem. Also, boys thrive on the approval of a loving father or father figure; a boy will react defensively and distance himself from a harsh disciplinarian or indifferent father, the very person he needs to be close to.

By showing, through love and rules, that you care, you help him to care about himself and others, including you.

37 Love him for who he is

One of the hardest things to do is to love and accept boys for who
they are. Instead, we dwell on what we see as their flaws and worry
about our dreams for their future. We worry that our hopes might be
dashed. But if you focus on an idealised future, the present will
always disappoint; and if you let your disappointment show, the
relationship that should fill your son with confidence will undermine
him instead.

Boisterous boys are like bear cubs. They are rumbustious, full of
energy, sometimes clumsy, and have an urge to explore, play and
tumble about. They are spontaneous, noisy, bubbly, irrepressible,
with a capacity for both fun and fury; but they also have the capacity
for deep and serious thought. Sensitive boys are calmer, more
measured and thoughtful, and prefer to watch, test and experiment
before they commit; but they are also capable of fun and spontaneity.

A boy may mis-time the humour, mistake the signal, mishandle his
strength or misjudge the moment, but his urge to react and assert
himself must be understood and nurtured.

Parents

* imagine your son has lost all the characteristics that irritate you: he tidies his room or toys, takes his shoes off at the door, volunteers to wash up, never forgets anything; be aware that if he becomes who you want him to be, his essential personality may have gone and he will have lost himself

* list all of his pluses and minuses; balance each negative characteristic with a positive one; then add more pluses than minuses to the list

* let him live in the present, not with your fears; he has many years in which to grow and mature before adulthood

Teachers

* if a student becomes a 'clone', modelling himself on you or an ideal, he is likely to find it difficult to take risks and handle making mistakes

* to help the younger child appreciate who he is, outline him while lying on paper on the floor, then invite him to fill in his shape with his characteristics

* ask older children to list 20 things they like to do, beside which they should add: the date when they last did them, a £ sign beside things that cost more than £3, an 'F' if they prefer to do it with a friend, an 'A' if alone, a 'P' if it needs planning, and an 'M/D' if a parent did it as a child, then they can tell a story about their interests and likes

38 Don't make approval conditional on good behaviour

One of the things prospective employers are wary of when they interview people for jobs is any applicant who curries favour, seeks approval, avoids disagreement and seems not to have faith in his own judgement. Anyone showing these signs is rejected, for insecurity and uncertainty are unhelpful in the workplace.

Of course, we all have times when we feel insecure, but some people feel it more than others and some are hampered by self-doubt most of the time.

The tendency can start in childhood. Boys grow strong inside when they feel approved of, loved and accepted for who they are. If an adult's approval is conditional, forthcoming only when a boy is being 'good', he will be forever looking over his shoulder, creating distance between his instincts and his actions. Always having to play to the parental gallery, he will soon lose sight of himself and never develop any sense of personal integrity.

Parents

• accept that he won't be perfect and that mistakes are not only inevitable but also important for learning

• see the funny side of his errors

• behaviour talks: he's not bad, just trying to say something; look behind any naughty behaviour for possible reasons

• disapprove of what he does, not who he is

• with an older boy, you can disagree with what he wants to do, yet still support his right to do it

Teachers

• be aware that reward systems for work and behaviour might lead unsuccessful boys to feel disapproved of

• show approval towards all students: respect, show interest in and talk to each one, not just the accommodating and successful ones

• involve all students in decision-making, to develop their independence and self-esteem, and to demonstrate that you trust and approve of their ability to make judgements

• show that you value a wide range of skills

39 Hear his complaints

When my mum picked me up from primary school, she used to stand talking with her friends for ages. I was tired, wanted her and wanted to be home. One day, I told her this. She said she hadn't realised, and changed straight away.

A very young child takes life as it comes; he knows no different and passes no judgement. But as his sense of self and his speech develop, he begins to reflect and see the world from his own perspective. He becomes aware of his own desires and wishes, and can form his own judgements. That's when he starts seeing that things can, indeed, be different; and when he puts this into words, he is expressing and risking his total experience of himself.

This is why, as soon as he is able to voice, or display, disappointment or dissatisfaction, his complaints should be taken seriously and responded to respectfully. His self-confidence and self-understanding depend on it.

Parents

* let him know that it's okay to complain: put a sheet of paper in his bedroom for written comments if he finds it difficult to face you

* listen to his complaint, for it could be his first step towards a compromise and an important lesson in conflict resolution

* try not to be defensive or competitive if he complains

* be ready to apologise if he says you have gone too far

Teachers

* turn any complaint into a question or statement: 'It sounds like you think this mark isn't fair because you tried really hard this time, is that right?', 'I think I need to explain myself more fully. Thank you for letting me know'

* if you are able to enter a student's world, see how things are for him and accept his perspective, you will be modelling empathy and teaching him emotional literacy

40 Acknowledge his disappointments

Disappointments are part of growing up. Boys have to learn that they can't always get their way, and that when they don't, life doesn't fall apart. We have to learn to compromise, and sometimes to do without.

If any parent sets out to make sure their son never experiences disappointment, he or she will end up being enslaved to him. He will not learn to live with and through setbacks, and it will not help him understand himself, because he will never have to decide which of a range of alternatives is really important to him.

However, there are times when disappointments matter a great deal, when they should be not only acknowledged but actively avoided. If the people your son needs to rely on and trust let him down frequently, it can lead to a profound sadness that may develop into depression or other mental health problems in later childhood or as in adulthood.

Parents

* try to predict when your son might feel disappointed

* don't ignore or dismiss his sadness

* talk about it; show insight and understanding by letting him know you know, and say something like: 'I know you'll be disappointed, but we can't go bowling until next week. I know you were looking forward to it. I'm sorry it can't happen and that I raised your hopes'

* it could be dangerous if he often feels that you have let him down, rather than simply disappointed at not being allowed to have or do things

Teachers

* most boys will feel disappointed if they get a poor result despite trying hard, though they may attempt to pretend otherwise

* try to acknowledge this when you give feedback, and if you think a student made a special effort, acknowledge this too; tell him not to be down-hearted and assert your confidence in his ability to take on the lessons to be learnt

* give him hope; discuss with him what he thinks needs to be done and what he can do differently, and end the conversation with a summary of steps he can take to improve his performance

41 Hold on to your authority

I thought I'd lost it. He wouldn't do a thing I asked. I felt completely useless, and became scared to have another go in case I got ignored again. Then I realised that, simply as his mum, I had all the authority I needed and I didn't need to prove it through shouting and screaming. I calmed down, thought ahead, decided on a few things I wanted him to do and stayed firm and fair. It worked, and we both feel so much better for it.

Adults have to find the right balance between staying in charge and getting caught up in power battles. Authority can be demonstrated in many quiet ways. Taking firm decisions about your family's or class's routine (i.e., what you do when), or what behaviour is right for your family, is one way. Being unflappable, and showing trust that boys will co-operate as asked or expected is another. When you take clear responsibility for deciding things, it is a demonstration of your authority.

Parents

* parents possess the authority that is vested in their position as parents; you may have lost touch with this, but can never lose it

* be aware that things like threats and bribes, or shouting and shaming, are tools of power that children resent deeply; they will ultimately undermine your authority, not boost it

* you demonstrate authority when you take responsibility for things

* take responsibility; if things have been going badly, tell your son that he hasn't been himself, and be constant about guidelines you set

Teachers

* if you trust a boy to behave as expected, and he in turn trusts you, this demonstrates your authority, and assumes a joint responsibility for resolving any problems

* if you make it clear from the start that your professional objective is every child's best interest, and you are able to convince him of this, he will not lose faith in you or in himself when you make a mistake

42 Use reasons to explain, not persuade

I'm not sure why, but the more I explain to my son why I want something done, the more likely he is to sit tight and refuse to do it.

Boys deserve to be given reasons: it shows respect for their right to know and respect for their ability to understand. Hearing reasons teaches them how to put forward an argument and to be rational. But it goes wrong so often. Why? The answer is that if you offer too many reasons, it changes what you say from an authoritative command to a much weaker exercise in persuasion.

First, children switch off at the first sound of a wheedling, pleading voice because they've heard it before, they know what's coming and they feel manipulated. Second, we weaken our case by overstating it. Children are smart, quickly see multiple reasons as a device to get them to agree, so they argue and refuse.

No more than two reasons are needed. All an adult needs to say is: 'This is what I want you to do, this is why, now go and do it.'

Parents

* give no more than two reasons to explain why you want something done

* look him in the eye as you tell him, so you come across as serious

* then turn away, because this conveys the clear message that you expect him to comply; hovering suggests he won't do it and will need policing

* to avoid appearing too controlling when you want to say no, ask him to guess and then tell you what your answer and reasons are likely to be

Teachers

* if a student asks for something outside the accepted rules, ask him to state his understanding of the rules and guess what your answer is going to be; he then gets to the answer 'no' without you having to say it

* use no more than two reasons to explain why a student has to do something

43 Be fun, fair and flexible

My grandfather grew up in a mining village where all the families had very strict rules. But for one day, once a year, all those rules were dropped. The children were allowed to do what they wanted, knock on elderly neighbours' doors and generally go wild. They let off steam and everyone had fun. It sounded great!

While many boys seem to enjoy the safety and security offered by structure, they won't thrive if they feel restrained by the unrelenting grip of a grim disciplinarian.

Whoever is responsible for him will gain a boy's respect and full co-operation only if the rules stay in the background, and his daily experience is, instead, characterised by fun, fairness and enough flexibility for him to feel he is listened to, loved and cared for as an individual.

Parents

- regularly set aside time for family fun, outings and games

- at birthdays, Christmas, etc., presents or chocolates can be hidden around the house as a treasure hunt to add to the fun, and it shows you have made an effort to do something special for them

- all children love family rituals, whether weekly, monthly or annual; if these can be fun, involving some relaxation of rules, they will be enjoyed even more

- flexibility, backed by a reason agreed with a twinkle in your eye, won't lead to any loss of authority; insensitive rigidity will

Teachers

- though curriculum planning and targets offer less room for flexibility, fun can be introduced into lessons through quizzes and games as alternative routes to learning

- try to see milder pranks as boys having fun and letting off steam; if you let them get to you, they'll do it again

- be creative: adapt a lesson to address an issue currently in the headlines

- being fair means not just treating everyone equally but also being sensitive to the reasons for an individual's behaviour or request

44 Rules cut conflict

Discipline is the aspect of parenting that causes most parents the greatest heartache. It is also the thing most parents feel they get wrong. This isn't surprising, because there is rarely a 'right' answer: the rules have to shift as boys grow and circumstances change.

Creating family rules is difficult because it entails balancing different people's needs and demands, managing different and developing personalities and sometimes compromising between different cultures and values.

However, it is clear that, provided they are agreed in advance and fully understood, family rules cut conflict. It's conflict that does the harm, not rules. Clear expectations and established daily patterns reduce the number of challenges. When your boy sees you mean business, he'll stop pushing you.

Parents

- conflict isn't avoided in the long term by giving in; he'll only learn that the more he pushes, the more he gets

- boys in particular like the security that rules provide

- being rule-abiding at home will help him to be law-abiding later

- be clear, be fair, be firm and be consistent; don't have too many rules, keep them simple, and stick to them nine times out of ten

- if you feel you're losing control, prioritise; stay firm on the issues you care most about and drop the rest

Teachers

- clear rules, applied fairly and consistently throughout the school by all staff, help children know where they stand and feel secure

- involve the boys themselves wherever possible in agreeing the rules so they don't feel so put upon and can take more responsibility

- have specific graded consequences for clearly defined breaches of the rules

45 Avoid wielding the tools of power

One friend of mine never stops talking about his father. It's never good. His father was a bully, sarcastic, critical, was alternately friendly and hostile, played him off against his brother, wouldn't accept any different point of view from his own. He did my friend no favours. He has now spent years trying to sort himself out, getting his confidence back, feeling comfortable with disagreement and learning how to be tolerant.

The tools of power that adults use are hitting, hurting, damaging belongings, bribery, ridicule, threats, sarcasm, shouting, emotional withdrawal and withholding food and liberty. It may be tempting to use these sometimes, especially when you are running out of steam, but it will be counter-productive. Boys will certainly find ways to get their own back, to preserve what they see as their self-respect

Our children deserve the best from us, not the worst.

Parents

* it is best not to force an issue when either you or your child is tired. Let it go, in case it blows up in both your faces

* try using the 'soft no'; if he does not respond to your request straight away, instead of raising your voice and issuing threats, repeat it more quietly, making sure you and he are looking directly at each other

* try trusting him to comply, giving one or two reasons, or using creative ways to get his compliance instead

Teachers

* responding with instant punishments in an apparently arbitrary way is an abuse of power; be measured, fair and consistent to avoid resentment and maintain students' co-operation

* avoid using sarcasm and ridicule in the classroom; these are not appropriate tools for confident, positive teaching

* don't react to challenges personally; doing so will lead to communication breakdown

* people shout and throw rulers when their patience and skills have run out; suggest that you team-teach to refresh your skills if you lose control more than occasionally

46 As the adult, it's your job to repair

My son and I couldn't see eye-to-eye. We had one patch when we didn't speak for nine months.

When things have broken down, however much you think your son is at fault, it's your job as the adult to mend your relationship with him. You have the greater wisdom, maturity, confidence and skill to achieve this. Refusing to acknowledge or communicate with your son is no way to teach him how to repair relationships or to give him confidence in himself.

Parents

* when your son's behaviour is awful, try not to take it personally; he will often be misbehaving to get attention or to protect himself, not to get at you, unless he feels he has good cause; you should not need to retaliate

* make the first move and take responsibility for the bad patch

* make the second, third and fourth moves; after a bad patch, trust is thin, so don't expect a quick turn around; conciliation should not depend on immediate reciprocation

Teachers

* personality clashes are a fact of life: some students seem to rub you the wrong way, but the onus is on you to sort it out; be open with the student, reflect on any past personal experiences that may explain your reactions and take responsibility; suggesting a different teacher may be the only way out

* be aware that personal and professional stress can undermine skills and tolerance; if you are under stress, be open about your state of mind, apologise, state your needs clearly and your class will almost certainly offer co-operation and understanding

47 Discipline without dictatorship

All boys need boundaries to help them control and manage their behaviour and to fit into a family or school framework of rules. Boundaries and rules help to keep boys safe, to fit in with and be acceptable to others, to show that you care about what happens to them and get you involved in their world

A framework of rules is essential for building self-esteem because it suggests that life will be structured, planned, predictable, have a rhythm and pattern, and be safe and positive. But only discipline which acknowledges and respects the needs of the child will achieve this. Discipline which is inflexible, which humiliates, in which the adult uses his or her physical, verbal and authoritative advantage inappropriately will, steadily and inevitably, chip away at a boy's self-esteem.

Parents

- be clear and prioritise; don't have too many rules and keep them simple

- be firm – but also friendly and loving; stick to your rules, nine times out of ten, but be flexible when it really matters to a boy

- be fair – because this is the best way to stop your son from becoming resentful

- be consistent: try to respond in the same way each time and get your partner to do the same

- keep your love constant: don't blow hot and cold

- set a good example: behave as you expect him to behave

Teachers

- dictatorship no longer works in the classroom (if it ever did); barrack-style orders and insults are no longer acceptable

- as with parents, be clear, be firm, be fair, be consistent, be fun and be flexible, giving reasons whenever you adapt or relax the rules

- plan for variety and use different teaching styles to engage all students naturally

- high expectations, clear rules and goals, suitably paced and engaging work, occasional humour and unfailing respect, are far more effective than threats, sarcasm or ridicule

48 Punishment without humiliation

My dad used to make me sit at tea with no clothes on when I'd been 'bad'. And he thought he was justified because he hadn't laid a finger on me. I've hated him ever since.

There are effective and ineffective ways to show boys how to manage their behaviour. When people use humiliating punishments, it rarely works.

For punishment to work well as a learning device, it should relate directly to the outcome, and not cause anger, bitterness or other bad feelings; in other words, it should be fair and leave a child's self-respect intact.

Any punishment which is designed to humiliate a boy will be felt as an attack on his person, not his behaviour, and will be counterproductive. Punishments which humiliate cause shame, guilt, self-doubt and ultimately self-hate. They lead to resentment, antagonism and hostility. Boys are not tougher than girls. To protect himself, a boy will ultimately cut himself off from the relationship and become uncooperative. Every put-down brings its own repercussions.

Parents

* if you use punishments, try to be clear, fair, consistent, brief, loving and sensitive to their effects

* deal with only one behaviour at a time – don't pile on the complaints

* punish the act and not the person

* alternatives to smacking include: withdrawal of privileges; restricted use of a favourite toy or pastime; withdrawal of pocket money; use of a cooling-off place; a verbal telling-off; and sending to bed early

Teachers

* always give due warning of any punishment you may give

* if your school does not have a behaviour policy, ask for one to be developed which contains clear and graded consequences for clearly defined behaviour

* don't up the ante if boys challenge you or feign indifference

* ensure the punishment fits the crime

* avoid taking challenges personally; when that happens, punishments become personal too

49 Model effective conflict resolution

Constant conflict ruins relationships and tears families apart. Children are deeply scarred by conflict, particularly when it becomes physical and involves both their parents. Family conflict lies behind much teenage despair that finds expression in depression and suicide.

But we can't get rid of all conflict. Different people inevitably have different and conflicting interests that have to be reconciled. Also, each of us has times when we feel exposed and vulnerable, when we are inclined to see comments and actions as challenges, take these personally and react aggressively, even where no challenge was intended. What we can do is to understand better why and when this happens, and how to manage and resolve the situation so that it does not get out of hand and those involved don't walk away feeling aggrieved, resentful, angry and ready to get their own back as soon as they can.

Resolving conflict safely and satisfactorily takes emotional maturity and skill. Children have to learn these attributes from adults.

Parents

• good communication skills lie at the heart of successful conflict management; listen to his case, present your case, using only 'I' statements, not provocative 'You' statements, and discuss compromises

• acknowledge the feelings and challenged interests underlying the dispute

• you don't need to win every battle; be prepared to walk away when the issue isn't critical, and avoid disputes when either of you is tired

• sibling battles teach children about conflict; if safe, let older ones resolve their problems; younger ones will need help

Teachers

• schools should adopt a clear policy of non-violence (see *Towards a Non-violent Society: checkpoints for schools* on **Reading List**)

• younger children can have a table where they go to talk through any dispute safely

• all school staff can be briefed about non-violent ways to resolve conflicts

• personal and social education programmes should contain lessons on violence prevention and effective strategies to manage and resolve conflict

• how teachers respond to challenges from children in class sets a powerful example

CHAPTER 6

Responding Sensitively to Setbacks

Life presents everyone, including children, with experiences that can knock them for six. It is part of every school and carer's job to prepare the boys in their care for these ups and downs. Being bullied or excluded from groups, families breaking up, friendships ending, bereavement or separations, and disappointments at school or on the sports field are common experiences. Children can't be protected from every possible hurt, however much parents may wish to and however desirable it may be – and it may not be. But how can adults help to rebuild a boy's self-esteem when all he wants to do is run away and hide?

Most of us will know a child who seems to be made of rubber and wears a permanent grin. Nothing seems to get him down. Whatever the problem, he has the ability to take the knocks, keep his attention fixed on a better future and make his way steadily, knowingly and confidently towards it. Such a boy is called resilient. He is able to live with and through adversity, getting himself back on course, ready to move on and even to use the setback to strengthen and enrich himself.

Recovery from difficulties is more likely when adults respond sensitively to a boy's setbacks. When they manage his confusion and dejection well, he retains enough self-respect and self-esteem to face the world again, have another go and treat the setback as an opportunity to grow and learn.

Resilience is sometimes described as the ability to 'bounce back'; however, this misrepresents what happens. Staying power involves action, not reaction. People with staying power think, feel, perceive and understand themselves and their situation in a way that enables them to remain positive, active and able to recognise the lessons to be learnt.

What gives boys staying power? Recent studies of children who recover from setbacks show that personality plays a small part, but more helpful factors are a tendency to see themselves in a good light, having at least one good, close relationship with an adult and not being exposed to too much difficulty.

Boys who bounce back have a good sense of their own worth and abilities, believe they can shape what happens to them, are able to live comfortably with uncertainty, are good at solving problems, mix well with others, can maintain friendships and are generally optimistic about life. Parents and teachers can help boys by encouraging this and responding sensitively to them.

50 Give him safe time to talk

After my parents split up, I went to my Dad every other weekend. The only time he asked me how I was was during the short journey home in the car. He wasn't really interested. He was making it safe for him to talk, not for me.

When boys feel close to someone and are able to make sense of what's happened to them, they are more likely to recover from setbacks. Talking usually helps, but the time and place must be right. There's no point in raising the issue in a place where the conversation will be overheard, where either of you feel uncomfortable, or when there's insufficient time to explore and come to some conclusion, even if it is: 'We need more time to talk'.

This is particularly relevant if your son is ashamed about what has happened or if he feels responsible – if he has been bullied at school or been found cheating or stealing, for example. Children sometimes feel they're to blame for things that are their parents' responsibility, such as relationship problems. Even if they don't believe they're the cause of the problem, they may still feel guilty for not having prevented it.

Parents

• avoid being intrusive; always check whether he's ready to talk

• make sure there is enough time before you begin talking

• make it clear from the start that the conversation is confidential, and get his permission to pass anything on to someone else; say: 'Do you mind if I tell Dad/Mum/your teacher what you've said?'

• if your son finds it hard to talk, try going out for a walk together; say you are ready to talk when he is, but leave the initiative to him

• be aware that boys sometimes prefer to work things out in their own heads rather than talk

Teachers

• befrienders' schemes are useful during primary and lower secondary school, and allow pupils to talk to their peers

• in the early secondary years, form teachers play a vital role – they should be selected for their proven abilities in dealing sensitively with pupils

• written references to personal issues or problems should be taken seriously and responded to sensitively, not ignored

51 Fortify his heart, don't thicken his skin

Many people believe that the best way to arm their son against verbal attack and disappointment is to thicken his skin, to get him to 'toughen up'. They achieve this in three ways. Some make a habit of speaking harshly to their son, just to get him used to being hurt, to create an immunity to it. Others constantly tell their son, because his emotions make him vulnerable to pain, he should deny or distance himself from them. Most commonly, people advise boys to hit back.

A far better way to protect him is to strengthen him on the inside – his emotions and belief in himself. The other route not only does great damage to a boy's self-esteem and self-understanding in the process, it also cuts him off from his essential self. Suits of emotional armour stop feelings coming out as well as going in, and therefore offer no long-term help with managing relationships.

Parents

• build his inner strength: trust him; see him as competent; let him have some autonomy over his life; respect his view of the world and tell him you love him

• if he's in trouble, help him; don't put him down or say: 'Why did you get yourself into this mess?'

• encourage him to follow and trust his instincts; 'encourage' means to give courage, to 'enhearten'

• give him assertive things to say to people who hurt others, like: 'I don't know why you need to say/do these things that hurt others' or 'I don't have to listen to you' and advise him to turn away; discuss possible strategies

Teachers

• constantly monitor the different ways in which you talk to boys and girls

• ensure that you don't speak more harshly to boys than to girls, believing that they are tougher and can 'take it'

• don't fall victim to expressing stereotypical views about girls or boys

52 Nurture his self-respect

A boy may feel more humiliated than a girl when he has a setback –
when he believes he has let either you or himself down – because
most boys assume they shouldn't get things wrong or show any
weakness. If and when the difficulty becomes public, he won't be
proud of the position he finds himself in. His self-respect will be
damaged – even if he is not really to blame.

Yet what he needs to pick himself up and face the world again is a
double dose of self-belief and self-respect. In other words, when he's
feeling down, he will have the least of what he most needs. Whatever
you feel about the incident, your primary role must be to help repair
the damage done and to leave him with enough self-respect to start
over again. Humiliating him won't work.

Parents

* he learns to respect himself when he sees that you respect him

* those who are frequently blamed/shamed find it hard to hold on to their self-respect; they can retain it if they are guided, sensitively, to right their wrongs without criticism or insult

* self-respect grows partly from being given responsibilities and carrying them out successfully

* boys who shirk responsibility and are allowed to ignore the consequences of theiractions find it difficult to hold their heads high

Teachers

* show respect for them, so they can respect themselves

* help them to see the good in themselves and in what they are able to achieve

* encourage independent learning so that pupils learn to trust and respect their own judgement and don't hold themselves back for fear of being condemned as failures by others

* encourage students to respect each other; always listen respectfully and share successes; ask them to relate one of theirachievements before they were ten, between ages ten and twelve, and so on, in small groups

53 Avoid shame and guilt

Shame and guilt are natural human feelings. When people have specific duties and responsibilities, and fall short of meeting them, it is natural that they might feel some shame or guilt. So why is it so important for a boy's self-esteem to protect him from too much shame, when the cry so often is that troublesome boys seem to be shameless?

Shame and guilt create confusion and self-doubt. They are difficult and destructive emotions for all children, largely because they mean they have let themselves or someone else down, and probably don't understand why or how. Occasionally, it is appropriate for a boy to feel shame and guilt – for example, if he's old enough not only to know how he should behave but also to manage his behaviour (and therefore to be held fully responsible for it). If, on the other hand, an adult stirs up shame and guilt in a boy to punish him, it's unlikely to produce the desired result. Rather than changing his ways, it is much more likely that he will reject these uncomfortable feelings and deny responsibility for the problem.

Parents

* make it clear that he is not to blame for any marital or relationship problems you are having

* if he has tried to sabotage a new relationship of yours, ask how he feels; don't play on his guilt

* address the consequences of his poor behaviour, not your shame or embarrassment

* if he is being bullied, discuss what he can do to stop it; don't tell him he's weak

* let your son decide how he feels about his wrongdoing; the choice of a suitable consequence is your decision

Teachers

* instead of rubbing a boy's nose in his mistakes, make your expectations clear

* something's wrong if you often make boys feel guilty

* sarcasm and ridicule rarely lead to greater effort, for the shame they engender undermines confidence

* don't punish the whole class for something only a few have done; this produces widespread resentment, not guilt in the few

* don't blame students for things that are your fault; boys are usually aware of a teacher's shortcomings, and are likely to react to them too

54 Offer extra closeness

When a boy experiences stress and difficulty, he will need the reassurance of the adults he depends upon even more. However, if his parents are angry or disappointed, they are more likely to withdraw than to draw closer to him. Children understand themselves through their key relationships – those they have with friends, family and professionals. If these supports disappear in his time of need, your son will doubt himself even more profoundly.

Not only will he lose confidence in himself and question his identity; he will also be further confused and unsettled by the altered behaviour of the people closest to him.

All changes are difficult for children. In times of change and trouble, try to stay close and be around more.

Parents

• changes that may upset your son can include: moving house; starting at a new school; illness in the family; bereavement; you starting a new relationship and difficulties in your current one

• depending on your son's age, you can try: talking to him as he takes a bath; sitting on his bed at night; sitting next to him while he watches TV; keeping him company as he walks to the bus stop; or giving him lifts in the car and chatting to him as you drive

Teachers

• spend time with him in a quiet corner

• ask him to help you with tasks

• find time to have short personal conversations

• keep reminding him that he can 'talk things through' with you, or suggest another person he might talk to (friends, parents, form teacher or befriender)

55 Help him see the lessons to be learnt

Don't despair, start to repair! Parents and teachers offer effective help when they remain non-judgemental and let a boy work out for himself what went wrong, or what he did wrong, and what he can do to move forward again in a practical and confident way. There is always something to be learned from a setback. Rather than playing the victim and blaming someone else, your son can take the opportunity to come through the experience stronger, wiser and more competent.

Be positive. Instead of asking: 'What will you avoid doing next time?' you can ask: 'What might you do differently next time?'

Not all setbacks will fit this model. If a child is feeling down because he has been bullied, had a fight in the playground, or been dumped by a girlfriend, he will not necessarily have done anything wrong. But there will still be conclusions to draw and the solution should lie with him. Problems should be reflected and acted upon, not recoiled from or removed by an over-protective parent.

Parents

• unravel and break down the problem; if something went wrong, there will be practical reasons why

• don't let your son attribute setbacks to his own general incompetence; setbacks should not be seen as unalterable omens of his future but as learning opportunities

• ask him what he thinks went wrong; don't tell him what you think unless he asks, or tells you he's happy to listen

• identifying the lessons to be learnt is energising; when he can see what went wrong, he will know how to put it right and regain control

Teachers

• making students aware of the control they have over daily life enhances self-confidence; ensure that planners and homework diaries are used regularly and effectively

• we find out about ourselves by taking responsibility; the aftermath of setbacks provides opportunities for this

• develop the habit in students of asking questions like: 'What are the lessons to be learnt?' and 'What have I learnt?' which both foster reflection

• if homework is missed, ask for a realistic plan to retrieve lost ground

56 Hear his side of the story

When children have setbacks, it is quite common for parents to become emotionally involved, and the danger is that they will take the situation far too personally and feel shamed by it. Try not to assume, before you have heard his story all the way to the end, that your son is at fault, and don't tell him off for putting you in a difficult position with, for example, the police or his school.

If he is upset about something you consider minor, try to see it from his point of view. Adults and children perceive things differently, so avoid applying your judgements unthinkingly. Saying things like 'Stop making such a fuss,' 'It will pass,' 'I can't understand why you're bothered by that,' won't help him get over something, whereas helping him to think through the problem will.

By listening to his side of the story, you show that you are taking him seriously and respect his point of view, are treating him fairly, and don't always assume the worst where he's concerned. All of this will help him to maintain his self-esteem.

Parents

• let him tell you about his disappointments, and don't belittle them

• assume the best of him, not the worst

• in arguments between brothers and sisters, listen to everyone's story, then ask each of them in turn to suggest a possible solution

• a child doesn't always want you to solve his problems; he may just want to sound off and be listened to; keep your opinions to yourself unless they are sought

Teachers

• don't assume he's in the wrong if he has a grievance against a teacher. Suggest he goes to the pastoral or year head to be heard and taken seriously in a neutral space

• hear his side of the story; avoid prejudice, stereotyping and hasty judgements; just because a boy has a reputation for causing problems, it doesn't mean he is implicated in this one too

57 Identify the danger signs and times

When Dale was fourteen, his parents split up. The separation was amicable and he seemed to cope well. But he soon became not only disorganised but also hypersensitive. For months afterwards, the slightest negative comment from classmates would result in tears and, if anyone laughed, he assumed they were jeering at him.

Children's resilience is obviously very low when their parents or carers split up, when someone close to them dies, and during other forms of family upheaval. But they are particularly vulnerable when they start or change schools – primary as well as infant and secondary schools.

Boys' confidence also drops when they pass through key developmental stages – at the age of about eight and at the onset of puberty and adolescence. At eight, they begin to think for themselves. In their second year of secondary school, 'macho' culture begins to take hold as male hormones kick in; boys gain more freedom through holding part-time jobs and stop trying to please. At these times, boys especially need a lot of attention.

Parents

* your son will need a lot of support and attention when he starts secondary school, and for the next two years

* situations that can destabilise children include:
  - domestic violence
  - racial abuse
  - constant criticism/abuse
  - home/school moves
  - divorce and separation
  - bullying
  - family re-formation, gaining step-families
  - bereavement
  - a parent's absence
  - family illness/disability
  - homelessness
  - being taken into care by the local authority/state

Teachers

* troubled children will often:
  - be withdrawn and lonely
  - be sad, prone to tears
  - fall asleep at school
  - have low concentration/be preoccupied
  - be reluctant to work or mix with others
  - be aggressive to others
  - be frequently bullied
  - be unable to follow routines
  - be clingy, dependent
  - need constant reassurance
  - contrive helplessness
  - cheat, lie or steal
  - destroy work on completion
  - destroy others' work
  - reject teacher's help
  - turn up late/be absent
  - be the class clown
  - be reluctant to state preferences/choices or agree targets

58 Deal positively with peer pressure

Peer pressure, along with bullying and drugs, is a subject that frightens many parents, and it seems that parents of boys are particularly worried about these issues. Quite apart from not wanting the expense of providing the 'in' trainers, designer leisurewear, and the very latest in computerised home entertainment, we like to believe that our sons will be sufficiently independent to withstand the pull of the peer group, especially when they become involved in illegal activities.

Children generally love to conform and hate to be different. Their earliest flirtation with independence from parents and self-expression is frequently via the safe route of fashion, and the younger they are when they choose their own clothes, music and so on, the more likely this is to be. Not all peer groups are insidious.

Parents

- don't drive your son into the arms of antisocial friends by being negative/constantly critical; the best way to help him resist them is to nurture his self-esteem and give him inner strength

- if he wants expensive clothes/games, facilitate his contribution towards their cost through saving regular pocket money or (if old enough) his part-time earnings

- ask him to question whether people who won't allow him to be different are truly friends

- remember, boys who are open to peer pressure are impressionable; help him feel that he is acceptable as he is

Teachers

- be aware of the power of peer groups to divert some boys from their studies; a befrienders' scheme can offer vulnerable boys a listening ear

- discuss the issue of peer pressure frequently in assembly, English or PSE lessons

- many boys who are seduced away from learning are vulnerable because they are already failing; identify those who might be led astray as early as possible and offer them mentoring to keep them on track

59 Keep him informed of developments

One of the most important needs we all have is to be kept informed about changes and events that affect us. We get very annoyed if employers, partners, the local council or neighbours do things without letting us know in advance. Children need to be told things too, especially if their families are going through changes.

If you are having a trial or permanent separation or going through a divorce; if someone in the family is ill and needs a lot of medication or has to go into hospital, perhaps for an operation; or if you are looking at possible schools for him, your son will want to know how things stand. All children can panic and think the worst, or disappointed by an unrealistic dream, if they have only sketchy information to go on.

As stated earlier, if you keep your son informed, you show respect for his right to know, his need to understand what's happening to him, and his ability to take in that information and use it sensibly.

Parents

* children should be kept informed about: events and changes (before, during and after they happen); feelings (yours and theirs); decisions and facts

* anyone who feels uncomfortable about raising issues such as going into hospital, dying, divorce or moving, can go to the library and borrow a children's book that explores the subject through a combination of fiction and factual information

* children need to make sense of their world and what is happening around them; keeping them informed of developments is an important way to do this

Teachers

* ensure that children know exactly why something is happening, from the very simplest reasons, such as what the aims of a particular lesson are, to why a pupil is being moved to a different group or who'll be taking the class while you are away

60 Find good support groups

When my mum died, my life fell apart. My friends at school and the swimming club were the two things that kept me going. The club got me out of the house and made me feel normal. My friends were just great.

Research into what helps children and young people to manage difficult personal experiences shows that they do better when they are involved in a range of groups and feel part of a wider community.

Belonging to a group can help boys because it:
- makes them feel secure about who they are when they might otherwise question their identity and their future;
- maintains continuity by preserving their normal daily and weekly patterns and routines;
- and gives them the understanding and support of people who know them and have time for them.

Parents

• help your son to attend his regular groups and clubs during troubled times

• if he has few commitments other than school, see if there are other activities locally in which he can become involved

• if he's having trouble at school, outside groups can help him start new relationships with a clean sheet

• this is a time when he may be drawn into undesirable groups, so keep an eye on him

• don't let your need for his company isolate him from his friends

Teachers

• encourage boys who are having a difficult time to sign up to lunch-time clubs and after-school activities

• vulnerable boys may benefit from being kept together in stable class groups to encourage security and support

61 Minimise conflicts at home

This is a hard one, for arguments are a natural part of family life. However, time and time again, conversations with boys have revealed how hard it is for them when home is, in their eyes, characterised by conflict. We also know from these conversations that violence and conflict in the home are associated with boys who have particularly low self-esteem.

Conflict is unsettling. When boys are going through a difficult time, and already feel unsettled, parents should take extra trouble to avoid arguments, both between themselves and with the boy concerned. When parents fight, verbally or physically, boys can feel under pressure to take sides, which splits them down the middle.

How can parents know when their family conflict is greater than 'normal'? Factors that make a difference include: frequency (of arguments; who is involved; what the disagreement is about; whether it becomes noisy or personalised; whether verbal or physical violence, abuse or bullying are involved; and whether and how the conflict is resolved.

Parents

* discuss cutting back on arguments during difficult times

* encourage everyone in the family to write down their complaints instead; these can be discussed at a set time, say, once a week

* be aware that personal insults, shouting and abuse will damage a boy's self-esteem

* discussion and debate are healthy; they are not the same as conflict

* teaching and modelling ways to resolve conflict will be of life-long benefit to your son

Teachers

* conflict at home, especially domestic violence, can affect boys' school work; it needs to be taken seriously at school

* discussions about why conflict happens, and how to resolve it, should be part of all personal and social education programmes

* if boys discover that others are coping with the same problems, it may help them to cope

CHAPTER 7

Supporting His Learning and Personal Growth

A boy who feels good about himself achieves good results, and tends to do well at school. Parents and other adults who support his learning and wider personal development give him a good head start and make him feel good about himself.

To be motivated to achieve anything, a boy must believe in himself. Self-esteem and a sense of self-worth lie at the heart of successful learning and growth. 'I believe I can do it' is as important as 'I want to do it'.

Boys feel capable when they are given opportunities to test themselves and be successful; when someone lets them know they have done well; when they have been understood, trusted and respected; when they feel physically and emotionally safe; when they feel accepted for who they are; and when others love them and enjoy their company.

If boys are punished and ridiculed; told off for trying new things, asking questions or making mistakes; constantly criticised; ignored and made to feel insignificant; or if an adult or teacher's expectations are so high that pressure and failure become unavoidable features of their lives, they will close themselves off, leaving their potential untapped.

Learning and growing involve change and taking risks, the unpleasant possibility of outright failure, facing up to limitations, and the excitement of discovering new talents. When boys feel competent and good about themselves, they are likely to be optimistic about their present and future skills and abilities. Confident boys with a sense of their own identity know their potential and therefore imagine who and what they might become. They see the unknown as exciting and a challenge.

Boys who are very unsure of who they are feel the opposite. Pessimistic about what they are capable of achieving, they tend to block out negative thoughts, sidestep failure and avoid change, claiming either that they know it all already or have no need to know. These are self-protection tactics. Boys use them to avoid challenge, which will move them on. Seeing learning as 'uncool' is simply one further, highly convenient and notionally respectable way of avoiding taking responsibility for success and failure.

Far too many boys so lack self-confidence that they cut themselves off from trying to succeed at anything. Many lack positive role models of successful men who can show them what they may achieve. Boys need to be shown the learning potential inherent in every failure and that they are capable.

62 Encourage and value a range of skills

A boy in London's deprived East End wanted to study Dance at A-level. A dance project at his school had given him a new interest and talent. When his father found out, he was furious. He threatened to throw his son out of the house if he went ahead, so the boy was forced to give up his dream.

Children do best when they experience lots of success and believe they are good at a range of different things. The more they experience themselves as competent, the more likely they are to have a go at new things. They will also widen their skills base, which will increase their ability to cope in a range of different situations. Academic success is by no means the only way to value a child.

Every boy will have many talents. He may be good at football, dancing, drawing, constructing models, climbing trees, rollerblading, or bicycle tricks. He may know a lot about insects, animals or gardening, be good at thinking things through or getting himself organised. He may be quick to understand how someone's feeling, or be tuned in well to his own feelings.

Parents

• try to broaden his base of achievement; let him try a range of activities and skills; libraries keep details of local children's groups and activities

• every child will benefit from believing he is good at something – it might be cleaning his bike, playing with other children, being creative with Lego or good at computers, for example

• limit television viewing; he needs balance and variety to get the best from himself and to feel proud and successful

• try to involve him in the practical things you do around your home

Teachers

• find something that each boy is good at, tell him he's good at it, and work to develop his strengths

• if a boy has a talent that is unusual, encourage the other children to respect his skill; but first, find what it is

• work hard to break down gender-stereotypical choices for options in Year 9

• set up after-school and break-time clubs to introduce students to new interests

63 Support and encourage, don't control and push

Support and encouragement give boys the energy they need to concentrate better, stay with things, achieve more and feel good about their progress. Controlling and pushing can leave boys exhausted, resentful and inclined to opt out.

When we support and encourage, we share a boy's burden and give him the courage to try new things. By contrast, when we control and push, we add to his burdens, imply that he cannot be trusted to do it on his own, sap his courage and undermine his self-belief.

Controlling, pushy adults are likely to finish tasks for their son; fill his time with activities; point out mistakes immediately; be competitive; issue threats; set new goals in quick succession; hover and get involved in homework, rubbing out mistakes and so on.

Parents

* show an interest in what he does; watch him undertaking various activities; ask how things went after he makes a special effort

* offer help, take him where he needs to go; discuss problems; answer questions

* listen when he tells you about his problems and successes; share his enthusiasm about dreams and goals; mark his achievements

* show trust; help him set his own goals in a time frame he can manage

* discover and accept your son's learning style and preferred work patterns

Teachers

* give him detailed information about the progress he's made and what he still needs to do

* help him devise a plan of action if he gets stuck, to keep him on course

* be enthusiastic about his improvements

* use stars, stickers and incentives carefully; if boys decide it's no longer cool to work for rewards, they are left with nothing to work for

* letters, postcards or certificates sent to students' homes remove the potential for peer ridicule and allow parents to enthuse about their sons' achievements

64 Trust that he'll manage

I sit with him every night when he does his homework, and then I check it. If it's no good, I make him do it all again.

We agreed with our twin sons when they were fifteen that they should start to save if they wanted to go to university. Both worked at weekends and holidays from then on, both did four A-levels, and both got four A's.

These two stories represent two very different attitudes to learning. One implies no trust, the other plenty of it.

Parents

* managing part-time jobs and school work is possible if handled sensibly; try it before you ban it; it can teach great time-management skills and is good for CVs

* when your son starts a new school, trust that he'll cope; saying: 'I hope you will/will not...' suggests you fear the opposite

* when he's trying something, let him know you believe he can do it, then walk away; don't hover over him expecting problems

* if he says he's ready for an exam or a test, don't push him to go through his revision once more

Teachers

* ask whether he thinks he can manage; if he says yes, support him in his decision

* occasionally present work as a challenge; more often than not, boys will strive much harder if told: 'Now, I'm not sure you'll manage this'; however, this tactic must be used only when you firmly believe a student can cope with the work

65 Make it safe to make mistakes

Your son will need masses of self-belief to make the most of his potential, but he won't have this if you jump on him every time he makes a mistake. Companies will be looking to employ risk-resilient people in the future, not frightened rabbits.

Mistakes are an essential part of learning. 'Everyone gets scars on the way to the stars,' wrote the songwriter Fran Landesman. The motto of one American IT company is: 'If everything you do is a success, then you have failed' – because mistakes are a sign of creativity and the ability to take risks. Mistakes are also useful. They shed light on the task in hand. They show what does and does not work, and what needs to be done differently. Mistakes tell a story, and it is the story we need to understand.

If you are afraid of making mistakes and try to deny them, you are sending your son an unhelpful message. Business today is error-tolerant, rewarding staff for managing their errors rather than punishing them. Love him for who he is, not for what he can do.

Parents

* admit your own mistakes and say what you have learnt

* let him notice his own errors; say: 'I can see two problems here, can you?'

* if his homework is careless, ask whether he's doing it in the best way, at the best time and place

* if he performs badly under pressure, make sure he isn't investing too much in results or worrying what you'll say

* if he makes more mistakes than usual, he may not understand something, hasn't worked hard enough, or isn't using the right method, or something is troubling him

Teachers

* be honest about your mistakes, state what you've learnt from them, and apologise for them if appropriate

* if a boy makes more mistakes than usual, it could be due to your teaching methods, or he's distracted or anxious about avoiding errors

* raise class awareness of attitudes to making mistakes by encouraging discussion, and note whether boys react differently to girls

* often boys respond best when involved in activities that include risk-taking; ask them to consider why they succeeded (if they did)

66 Have realistic expectations

My six-year-old son's report was positive about every aspect of his work and social development. When I said 'Well done', he turned away and choked, 'It was a stupid report. What's the point of telling me I'm good when it's so easy?'

People perform according to expectation. They tend to live up to – or down to – their reputations. Far too many children have failed for far too long simply because they were not asked to do any better. They never realised what they could do because they had never been stretched, and they believed the limits of their capability to be those implied by the easy targets set. But parents and teachers have had it so drummed into them that they must raise their expectations to raise boys' performance that we're in danger of going too far the other way.

A target that is set too high is as unhelpful as one set too low. Challenges must tempt your son, not threaten him and put him off. Targets that are too high can lead to failure, shatter his confidence and make him believe that succeeding is the only way to gain your approval.

Parents

- ask him what he thinks he can manage

- help him to devise clear plans for meeting his goal

- invite him to think ahead about any problems he might meet and how he'll manage any setbacks

- invite him to select short-term targets, which seem more achievable, as well as a few longer-term ones

Teachers

- make sure the target, time and quality conditions are clear

- encourage planning and reflective skills

- let the boys assess whether the conditions have been met

- ask for a detailed study plan if you detect over-confidence – don't tell them that the target is unrealistic

- ask whether they're ready for the next challenge, or want some time to consolidate what they have learnt

- be clear, practical and realistic about your own targets

67 Read and learn together

Boys are known to lag behind girls in speech and language development, and this often has a knock-on effect on their interest and skill in reading. Children need to grow up in their own way and at their own pace, and there is no value whatsoever in pushing a boy to read if he is not ready to do so. However, all children find learning to read easier if they are familiar with books, are interested in what what they can learn from them, enjoy just looking at the pictures in them, and associate books with a cosy intimacy with people they're close to.

Grandparents, parents, aunts and uncles, stepfathers, stepmothers, boyfriends and girlfriends are all people who may have a special relationship with a boy and can help him start on the track to reading and fluent literacy by sharing books with him.

Parents

● boys are often more interested in non-fiction than in stories; information books don't have to be read from cover to cover; let your son choose, but be aware that for boys, reading fiction develops reflection and is enormously beneficial

● don't push him to read before he shows an interest in learning

● if fathers and other male carers find time to read to boys regularly, books are less likely to be regarded as 'sissy' or 'just for girls'

● avoid doing reading practice at bedtime – he'll be far too tired to concentrate

Teachers

● choose a range of subjects for class reading to appeal to both boys and girls, and recognise the learning advantages of reading fiction

● develop paired/shared reading programmes so that unconfident but competent readers assist weaker ones

● invite local male role models to class to discuss books, poetry and drama

● encourage a school culture that depicts reading as both a male and female activity

● set up seminars in junior schools at which boys present books they have recently enjoyed

68 Show an interest, but don't be intrusive

In all my years at school, my father never once came to a parent–teacher meeting, to watch a match or see me in a play. He reckoned he'd done his bit by earning the money to pay the bills. It cut me up, and I ended up dropping out.

This boy had successful parents. His mother was interested but his father wasn't. He clearly wanted both parents to know about everything he did that was special and significant to him. It doesn't take much to show that we're interested. It takes a question or two to initiate a conversation and follow up a point, a small moment out of the day to make a connection with a boy's life and thoughts. It does take more to attend evening meetings, especially if it means leaving work early, but putting yourself out and being there for him will make him feel that he's important to you and that you take his school and his learning seriously.

Adults can take this too far, however. They may ask too many questions and become intrusive.

Parents

• ask the right questions for the right reasons, directly, or leave well alone; don't try to get information deviously, because he'll almost certainly guess what you're up to, then shut you out

• wait for him to tell you about test results; don't ask about them straight away

• when he comes home from school, instead of asking what happened, you can tell him what you did, then say: 'Is there anything you want to tell me about your day?'

• questions about getting into trouble, or what he did at break-time, speak volumes about the issues on your mind

Teachers

• for secondary school parents' evenings, don't rely on 'pupil post'; use the official post or telephone to ensure that all parents have the opportunity to attend

• at parents'/new intake evenings and in school newsletters, constantly stress the important role that parents can play

• stress that, with boys, a positive role model is vital

• find time to take an interest in certain personal things that are important to the boys you work with most closely, but step back if any of them seem uncomfortable about it

69 Develop perseverance: help him to see tasks through

Boys have a particular problem with seeing things through. Girls are more persistent, dogged, and dutiful about doing things they have been asked to do, even if they find the task boring. They seem to be able to wait longer for a reward. Boys become bored more easily, and are less inclined to put up with poor-quality teaching or coaching that does not provide variety and stimulation.

Perseverance – or 'stickability' – is important. The best-laid plans can come to nothing without it. The motivation may be strong, and the target may be clear, but if a boy doesn't have the stamina to stay the course when he comes up against an obstacle, the work he has already invested may be wasted.

Boys may give up easily because they lack confidence. If you recognise this pattern, build up their self-belief at every opportunity.

Parents

• if he gets stuck, don't belittle or hand him the answers, but lead him so that he can find them himself and gain confidence to try next time; then back off

• when he shows signs of flagging, take an interest in him and ask him to read to you, show you what he's done, or tell you what he has enjoyed and found difficult

• if you use rewards, offer small short-term ones, not a big one a long time away in the future

• ensure that targets are reachable in his eyes, and that he makes a feasible plan

Teachers

• boys need work, and rewards, delivered in short, sharp chunks; keep all targets in clear view, with clear routes to each one, so that their interest does not wane

• if a student gets stuck or loses interest in a project, jointly prepare a plan of re-engagement

• delay work that requires deeper concentration until later in the lesson, when the boys' interest has been sharpened

• introduce variety into lessons and divide them into defined phases; include hands-on activities, quizzes and regular summaries of what's been achieved in each phase

70 Support the school

Boys, as we have seen, are growing up in a male culture that questions the value of social and academic success. No single person can change that culture. What we can do to encourage boys to believe that it's cool to succeed, however, is strengthen the ties between home and school, and support each other.

If parents respect schools, and schools respect parents, there will be fewer cracks for boys to fall through, particularly during the earth-moving time of adolescence. Parents who distance themselves from their son's school and its events not only create split loyalties, but also make it easier for boys to team up with the tearaways rather than the teachers.

Parents

• avoid complaining about your son's school in front of him, even if you're unhappy with it

• wherever possible, both parents should attend meetings about a boy's progress in school; the absent parent should telephone his teacher for a summary

• try to make time to watch him take part in school events; avoid saying: 'Not another thing that school/club/you want me to do!'

• attend fundraising events with your son so that he feels part of the school

• help him gather/remember the things he's been asked to bring to school

Teachers

• let parents know when things are going well, not only when there may be problems, so that they can feel proud of their sons and therefore good about themselves

• take parents' worries seriously, and respond to their concerns with respect

• avoid appearing to criticise a boy's parents: 'Didn't your mum know you'd need sandwiches for today's trip/check that you had everything?'

• make parents' evenings focus on what parents can do to help their boys set and achieve realistic, short-term targets in learning

71 Respect his teachers

It's far harder now than when I started teaching twenty-five years ago. It's not so much the constant changes to what we're expected to teach or the extra paperwork; it is the parents and the students who show us so little respect now. When children hear parents doing us down at home, it's hard for them to accept our authority and take work seriously when they're here.

Schools and parents need to work in together as partners – with each other, not against each other – if children are to do well.

Children need to trust their teacher if they are to engage fully with learning. Constant carping about teachers at home, especially about a particular one, will encourage a boy to block out whatever that teacher is trying to impart.

Parents

• at all times, try to reflect the teacher's commitments and perspective, even if you take your son's side

• teachers are people too; they have personal lives and sometimes go through hard times; they like to hear good news as well as bad; most do their best and are stretched close to their limit

• don't be too shy to tell teachers what seems to work best for your son; they can't know everything

• it's only fair to the teacher and your son to tell the school if there's a problem at home that might affect his behaviour or work in school

Teachers

• these days, we all have to earn the respect we feel is our due; don't put parents down; try to see things from their point of view

• be aware that vulnerable parents are likely to take your treatment of their son personally, as if you're doing it to them; respecting every boy in your care contributes to respectful home–school relationships

• send home good news, not just bad

• at parent–teacher evenings, take parents' concerns seriously, and end with: 'Is there anything else?'; an alternative time can be arranged if the issue demands it

72 Channel competition creatively

Almost all boys have a competitive urge. Channelled sensibly, sensitively and creatively, it can be used to good effect in developing their motivation, their capacity to achieve and their sense of self. Exploited carelessly, it can lead to anxiety, despair and a decision to opt out.

Boys will do best when they are encouraged to compete against themselves, when they focus on doing better than their last best effort. This way, their self-esteem can remain intact. The danger comes when they try to perform to impress their friends or adults, set their sights on beating others, and invest their self-worth in the result. Even though a boy may have tried really hard and prepared well, others might have tried harder, or simply have a more natural talent. Whenever the outcome is not wholly in his control, there is the chance that he'll fail because of anxiety, and his self-esteem may suffer.

Parents

- it is better to identify a specific target – 'Try to improve the mark for your piano scales' – than the general – 'Go for a distinction this time'

- don't fuel competition between brothers and sisters; each child needs to be successful in his or her own way, and accepted unconditionally for who he or she is

- avoid competing against your son, especially if your intention is to spur him to greater effort

- fun competitions are fine: 'See if you can beat me to the top of the stairs' is a great way to get him to go to bed

Teachers

- research shows that teaching based on competition produces anxious children

- encourage children to perform to improve, not impress, and give feedback to them so that they can see what progress they've made

- try playing musical chairs in two ways: first, as usual – removing chairs and children each round – and second, telling the children to find other laps as chairs disappear; ask which version they prefer; cooperative games show how much fun it can be just to join in

73 Failure lights the route to success

All boys experience failure – lots of it. A boy will almost certainly fail when he first tries to walk; he won't master buttons on his first attempt, ride a bike or tie his shoelaces straight away, yet he is prepared to have another go. Why is it that these early failures don't make growing boys give up, despite sometimes intense frustration, while later ones can stop them in their tracks and throw them into the depths of misery?

The uncomfortable truth is that adults are often responsible for the change. They start telling children off for failing, teasing them, and making them feel ashamed.

But failure is not something to be shunned. It provides factual and neutral information on what went wrong and what needs to go right. Failure is an inevitable and essential part of learning, and shows that learning is happening at the frontier of current knowledge. If the lessons to be learnt from failure are taken on board, they will light the path to success. This will not happen if adults deny, ignore or punish failures, making a boy feel he should hide and ignore the truth.

Parents

- respond constructively: failure is like a puzzle to be solved, not a disaster to be denied; consider whether the target was too ambitious

- respond genuinely: be honest about the outcome, and ensure it remains his problem, not yours

- respond sensitively: however much he may deny it, failure is upsetting and can undermine confidence; accept, understand and let him voice his feelings; don't be too strict with him; seek success elsewhere to balance a failure

- show that you love him for who he is, not what he can do

- don't punish him for failing – he may start to lie or cheat

Teachers

- describe in detail what went wrong and how to do better

- let him know you believe he can improve and demonstrate this with a sample piece of work

- encourage him to self-evaluate as much and as accurately as possible

- be available if he needs help

- look for modest, not unreal, success stories: individual boys can explain how, and perhaps why, they turned themselves around

- find out what might lie behind any unexpected fall-off in performance

74 Watch him doing something he enjoys

I lived for football. I played a lot and got really good, being goalie for a man's team when I was fourteen. My dad lived too far away to watch me, but my mum didn't come either. Being in goal's a big responsibility. It got too much. I couldn't tell the team how I felt. After two years, I quit. I was too stressed.

Anything that is important to us, we want to share. Children are the same. Children usually enjoy doing the things they do well, so one reason to watch them is to let them show off a little and accept the pride they feel in their achievement. Watching involves you further in your son's life; it increases togetherness even when he's doing something on his own. Your presence will boost his self-esteem.

If your son loves playing football, riding bikes or conquering playground equipment, watching certainly takes effort and may involve getting muddy, cold or wet. You may be mystified by his passion for strange, war-based, card or computer games. But he will thrive in the warmth of your watchful eye.

Parents

* find the time to watch

* 'Mum, can I show you how I...?', or 'Dad, come and see me do...' should be answered with: 'Sure', but preferably not with 'later' added

* let him impress you; tell him afterwards how much you enjoyed watching him

* within his hearing, tell his grandparents how well he's doing, so that he can feel pride in his skills; if they are no longer with you, you can say: 'Granny would have loved to have seen you do that'

Teachers

* you can't watch what the boys and girls in your class do in their personal time, but you can find a moment to hear about something they have done

* try to value whatever it is a boy enjoys doing or achieving

* provided that your family and work commitments allow for this, it can be gratifying for students to see other teachers attending plays, football matches, concerts, etc.

75 Don't invest your self-worth in his success

Every time I did well at something, my mum would rush off and tell the whole neighbourhood. She treated it as her achievement, and I ended up feeling used, empty and angry.

Although parents and teachers are naturally pleased when their sons and students do well, it is very dangerous when adults begin to rely on a child's success for their own sense of self-worth.

It can damage a boy's self-esteem in a number of subtle ways. If parents feel good about themselves only when their child succeeds, they are, in effect, stealing success from him; this will leave him feeling used, confused and empty instead of fulfilled. Only further, and repeated, success will restore his sense of achievement, which often leads to the burden of perfectionism. He will also come to believe that he is valued solely for what he can do, not for who he is.

Parents

- if you want to tell other people about your son's achievements, ask his permission; then think about who you want to tell, and why

- avoid setting your son a new target as soon as he has reached one; might you benefit in some way from the pressure you're putting on him?

- ask yourself whether you have higher expectations for your sons than for your daughters; do you identify more closely with your son for some reason?

- remind yourself it's his success, from his effort, and that it's his to hold on to

Teachers

- good teachers deliver more than results; to stop yourself becoming too hooked on results at times when you're at the risk of doing so, list some other things you are keen for your students to develop and achieve

- if you think you may become success-dependent, list all the other things you are good at which give you pleasure

- if one group's results are not good, and you find yourself becoming depressed as a result, put yourself back in control; list the things you could do differently next time that might change the outcome

76 Let him be responsible for his success and failure

The moment of victory is far too short to live for that alone.

MARTINA NAVRATILOVA

Success and failure tend to be overlaid with moral significance: it is considered good to succeed and shameful to fail. Parents can become infected by this way of thinking so that, if their son succeeds, it is their success and, if he fails, it is their failure. This can be damaging as well as confusing.

When parents 'own' their son's success, it is effectively stolen from him and it may lead him to fail in the future. They may do it to make themselves feel good, and run to tell others the good news, or they may take credit for his success, implying that he couldn't have done it without them. Either way, if success is always taken away, a boy may eventually turn on his tormentors and refuse to play, or burn out through his own perfectionism.

Taking responsibility for his failure is equally unhelpful. A parent's shame may lead to punishment or to trivialisation. Because the son does not take responsiblity for his errors, he will be unable to progress.

Parents

• have realistic expectations and accept him unconditionally

• see success as neutral feedback; it shows what he's doing right; glory shouldn't come into it

• help him feel comfortable with his feelings of delight or disappointment, frustration or sadness

• if his failures become your personal shame, you hinder his chance to learn lessons

• a failure is a sign that he's at the frontiers of his knowledge; discuss why it happened and what he can do differently next time

• your son's success is his; don't steal his thunder by taking credit for his success

Teachers

• always congratulate a student on his success, and give him credit for it

• describe in detail what he did right and the things that led to his success, so that he knows how to repeat it next time

• offer some unpressured time at his new level, with time to adjust to and accept his success; then allow him to move forward

• take the shame out of failure; it merely tells him what he needs to do differently; personal insults will encourage him to hide behind excuses

CHAPTER 8

Encouraging Confidence and Independence

Management trainers say the world is made up of three types of people: those who make things happen; those who watch things happening; and those who notice nothing until afterwards, and then ask, 'What happened?' Children who develop sound confidence are more likely to fall into the first category when they become adults. If you make things happen, you control your own life. The ability to manage independence creatively and safely gives us tremendous advantages.

But confidence, of course, ebbs and flows. We may feel confident in some situations, and terrified in others, relaxed with some people and uncertain with others. This largely depends on what we feel we're good at and how well we know the people we're with. Apart from these fluctuations, confidence also dips naturally at certain stages of child development, which happen at different times for boys and girls.

Two reports about this, entitled *Can-Do Girls* and *Leading Lads*, found that boys' self-esteem is a picture of extremes, with more boys than girls in the highest and lowest self-esteem groups. Girls showed a stronger thread of confidence running through both the medium-range and exceptionally confident *Can-Do* groups, but there are more *Can-Do* boys than girls (25 to 21 per cent). Boys in the middle group are more insecure, and there are also more boys than girls at the lower end (12 to 8 per cent). Boys are most confident at 14 (when confidence plummets for most girls) and least confident at 19.

Today very mixed messages go to children so that when they are small, they often get responsibility and power before they are ready for it, at a time when parents should remain in command. However, during adolescence, just when they need to feel confident and to be wresting control into their own hands, we tell them that it is a frightening world out there and, in effect, that they cannot be trusted to cope by themselves.

If, while he is a boy, you show trust and confidence in him, and have provided an emotionally safe, predictable environment for him, he won't become isolated during adolescence when uncertainty and self-doubt can make socialising painful. While most of us have times when we want to be alone or manage things by ourselves, spending too much time avoiding people and problems can distort boys' sense of reality and ultimately dent their courage.

77 Offer him safety, security and predictability

The Concise Oxford Dictionary defines confidence as 'firm trust; assured expectation; boldness'.

Nobody can develop self-confidence if he neither trusts himself nor has the assured expectation that other people's behaviour is trustworthy and predictable. Boys who do not have a measure of consistency and predictability in their lives will find it very hard to acquire the necessary trust – in others or in themselves – to become either truly self-confident or genuinely independent. When adults behave in an arbitrary and neglectful way, they undermine a child's confidence and generate emotional dependency.

Routines help to nurture both trust and security. If a boy's key carers clearly trust him and provide consistency, he can begin to trust himself, his judgement and the behaviour of other people. Parents don't make their son independent by disappearing from his life and letting him fend for himself, but by being there for him.

Parents

• ask yourself whether your son will begin each day with a clear idea of what's going to happen and when, in terms of routines, events, or people with whom he will be involved

• try to ensure that he sees any absent parent regularly

• make your own behaviour towards him as reliable and predictable as possible; if you have moods, or your routine has to change, try to explain why

• consider whether there's anything you can do to increase a sense of order and 'assured expectation' in his life

Teachers

• boys benefit when lessons have a clear structure and purpose, and the aims and objectives are made clear at the start, so they know what to expect

• boys work best when given tightly structured tasks that channel their speaking and listening energies and skills in purposeful directions

• let them know well in advance if there are to be any changes to the normal school day or lesson

78 Nurture his social skills

Boys, typically, tend to have less well-developed language, social and communication skills than girls. They are born more restless than girls, and are likely to find it more difficult to control their thoughts and behaviour, preferring to express themselves through action rather than words. They find it harder to understand or explain the reasons for their own or other people's behaviour; yet it is this reflection that encourages tolerance, compatibility and emotional literacy.

Increasingly, employers are looking for good social skills in job applicants. They want people who are happy to forge a range of relationships, who can work together in teams, who can discuss and sell their ideas and develop the empathy and understanding to manage disagreements. The ability to behave in this way lies at the heart of successful and comfortable working and socialising.

Socially adept boys who make and maintain close relationships are less likely to get into difficulties when challenged. Boys need help to express themselves honestly and safely – through words rather than physical aggression or withdrawal.

Parents

* involve him in your social life whenever appropriate to show you like being with him and trust him to be sensible

* try to be sociable yourself; if he sees you mixing confidently with others, he'll learn from you

* encourage friendships: invite his friends round, see if there's a social or sports group he can attend regularly; limit solitary activities like computer games

* reading will develop his ability to reflect and empathise; talk to him as much as you can; ask for his views; tell him what you've done; and listen properly to him when he talks to you

Teachers

* include paired and small-group work in your lessons so that boys learn to listen, talk, respect and compromise

* in mixed classes, ensure that boys work with girls, to pick up alternative ways of thinking, doing and learning

* seating arrangements are important; it can matter a lot to boys who they sit next to

* encourage discussion, listening and reflection; when boys develop these skills, and think before they write, the standard of their work rises

* invite local sports or pop stars to come and discuss favourite books, poetry and drama

79 Offer him opportunities to test himself

Confidence flows from competence. When a boy feels he can do things well, when his experience of himself is of one of success and overcoming obstacles rather than failing and falling short, his confidence will grow in leaps and bounds.

The more skills he acquires the better, but he won't achieve anything if he just watches TV all the time or is constantly told that he's useless. Get him out and about as well, to ensure a good balance in his leisure activities. Avoid gender stereotyping when you suggest new things he could try.

When the time is right, letting him have a taste of the world of work will help to increase his confidence about his possible future and let him see you functioning in a different role outside the home. He may wish to take some part-time work or, if it's relevant or feasible, he could occasionally go with you to work. Schools increasingly organise work experience for their students, but extra tasters before and after such placements will add to the benefits.

Parents

• every journey begins with a first step; he won't be as good as you, but he'll need to feel competent from the beginning; teasing him for incompetence will set him back

• activity holidays and after-school clubs can introduce boys to a range of new skills

• involve him in the jobs you do – cooking, cleaning, car washing, weeding, DIY, doing your business or home accounts, or caring for others – and be tolerant of the extra time it may take

• let him try out his thoughts and opinions on you and respect them; don't compete

Teachers

• boys need to be encouraged to volunteer for jobs, and special ones sometimes have to be created for them as an additional incentive

• encourage any boy who seems to lack friends, confidence and social skills to socialise in a variety of ways

• drama can be used effectively in many lessons to get boys to try out new roles and learn new skills

80 Work to and from his strengths

Any boy will learn more easily, perform better and be more self-motivated if he can do things in a way that suits him (using sight, sound or touch, for example), and through subjects that interest him. A child's all-important sense of mastery – how effective and competent he feels – will develop best when he is allowed to start from who, and where, he is.

Success breeds success. All educators know that when a child is good at one thing, his new confidence will help him to do better elsewhere.

Starting from the strengths your son has not only validates him but also demonstrates the vital unconditional acceptance which gives a boy the freedom to learn and develop in his own way. The more you ignore his preferences and impose your own, the more likely he is likely to lose touch with himself.

Parents

- identify his skills and strengths: concentrate on what he can do, not on what he can't

- don't belittle any talent that he values

- think about his preferred ways of working and learning, and his particular passions; don't force him to work in ways that go against his natural inclination

- if poor concentration is stopping him from reading fiction, you could: read the first few chapters to help him get into a book; try a series (the characters and story lines will soon become familiar); or short stories – science fiction, for example

Teachers

- boys like being adventurous, taking risks and performing to show off their verbal wit; Drama uses these talents, and can be a route to enjoying English

- discover a pupil's passion; apply it to your subject, and let him fly: boys concentrate better when they're interested

- quizzes are great favourites among boys: they challenge and feed their competitive instinct

- young boys' play often seems more vigorous, less verbal and fluent than girls'; build on it, don't stop it; encourage the development of story lines and characters using toys, models and, sometimes, girls

81 Independence without abandonment

Independence should be given to children as and when they are ready, and not be granted solely because it is convenient for an adult, regardless of whether it is appropriate to the boy's age, maturity and wishes. Sometimes, a family's practical needs are the catalyst for granting further independence, and it comes at the right time. However, it is important to judge whether your son's extra freedom is simply a convenience for you, and to be aware how he may view your motives. He should not be given too much too soon, exploited, or left feeling abandoned. Although he may appear to be able to cope, in reality he may still feel he needs your company, guidance and attention, but be too proud to say so.

If a boy feels put upon, used, exploited and abandoned, or uncomfortable with the extra responsibility that goes with greater freedom, his self-reliance and self-esteem may be damaged, not enhanced. He may feel anxious and out of his depth, which will increase any residual self-doubt and destroy his confidence.

Parents

• the first few times he does something new, stay close by or within easy reach, so that he knows he's not entirely on his own

• apply the idea of 'supported independence' to check whether he feels abandoned; friends may be able to provide this support

• ask him if he's truly happy with the arrangements you have made for him to travel, cope or be by himself

Teachers

• 'independent learning' is important, but students will continue to need support

• boys need help with time management; for projects with a deadline, schedule times when you will be available for consultation well before the delivery date

• suggest that students divide their work into 'bite-sized' chunks; deadlines can be set for sections to help steer them and to prevent anyone from falling behind

• tasks and responsibilities should carry clear guidelines

• ask what help a boy thinks he may need on solitary projects

82 Monitor and supervise
   – from a distance

One night I was due home by eleven. My friends and I cooked up other plans, so I phoned home with some made-up story about why I needed to stay the night with one of them. Mum just did not buy it and stuck to her guns. Afterwards, I was glad. I realised I wasn't sure what might have happened that night.

All the research shows that boys who get into trouble stay out for long periods of time without having to report their comings and goings to anyone at home. Monitoring and supervision help to keep boys on track when they are exploiting their new-found freedom, but it should be done sensitively and from a distance so that they don't feel insulted by any perceived lack of trust.

Being aware of your son's movements is vital. It helps to keep him safe because he knows you're aware and that you care. If you leave him to his own devices, he may flounder, feel neglected and then get his own back by actively looking for trouble.

Parents

- each time he goes out, discuss and agree times for calling in and coming home; when he comes in, casually ask him what happened and how things went

- if you are worried, check his story with his friends' parents; make sure you have their phone numbers

- follow it up if he's late, so he knows you've noticed, and you care; try to be awake on his return so you can judge what condition he's in

- check the atmosphere of the place where he hangs out and get to know his friends

- keep a regular eye on his bedroom; it will give clues to work or personal problems

Teachers

- be alert to any pattern in missed deadlines; consult with colleagues if you are worried

- closely patrolling children won't help them learn to manage and monitor themselves; keep an eye open at break-times, but from an appropriate distance

- records of marks for class and homework, lateness, and major incidents of bad behaviour are easy to keep; keep track of other less obvious signs of personal trouble, too, such as tears, visits to the school nurse and changes in personal appearance

83 Develop responsibility and safe risk-taking

Research shows that, from birth onwards, boys are more inclined towards risk-taking than girls, less reflective about any implications and therefore less thoughtful and cautious. Safer risk-taking can be encouraged by letting our sons know we care, by improving their thinking and reflective skills and, crucially, by ensuring that their responsibilities grow in line with their rights. Responsibility is important. Through it, we find out what we can do, we feel trusted, trustworthy and respected, and we gain in competence, which in itself contributes to safer risk-taking.

A boy should grow up with appropriate and increasing experience of responsibility, beginning with things like tidying up after himself, getting his school things ready and rinsing out his football and swimming outfits and equipment. Later, he can take reasonable and progressive responsibility for others, which also encourages task commitment. Nevertheless, the ability to take risks is important. Be tolerant of the mistakes your son will inevitably make while he's learning to take responsibility.

Parents

• when your son asks for more independence, try to give it to him; if the particular freedom he seeks causes problems, discuss an alternative change that will satisfy him – he'll then have less need to struggle and prove himself

• be aware of his co-ordination skills and physical strength, and keep his risk-taking in line with his physical abilities

• rights matched by responsibilities can encourage safer behaviour, but all boys, especially adolescents, will take risks at some point; talk to your son about safe risk-taking and trust, and set clear limits to his freedoms

Teachers

• learning involves taking responsibility and risks; when kept in balance, these offer useful lessons for life

• challenging boys, or those with low self-esteem, may respond well to being given special tasks and responsibilities

• boys who undertake death-defying acts may be mirroring the irresponsibility they perceive in close adults; be attuned to the reasons behind high-risk behaviour

• address the pros and cons of risk-taking in PSE lessons and assemblies; explore the need for thrill and excitement and the role it plays

84 Encourage self-management

When the parents of our new Year 7 intake first come in to school, they get the talk about how to beat the macho boy culture that so often takes hold. We discuss how they can help to resist it, and one of the first things I say is, 'Stop doing everything for him – get him to cope and manage on his own.'

It can be hard to let go. With such busy lives, we may feel we have fewer ways to demonstrate our love and commitment. One remaining way, as our sons grow up and become harder to hug, is to tend to their needs. Teachers say that boys start secondary school noticeably less independent and competent than girls, which affects their ability to study. We may unconsciously feel uncomfortable teaching boys to use the washing machine, cook or iron. Boys can be so clumsy, too. We'd rather do the job for him than see him struggle, mess it up or go out looking scruffy or without something because he's forgotten to think ahead.

But it is not helpful to mollycoddle boys. It keeps them dependent and stops them developing the skills they need for managing school, work and time.

Parents

• encourage financial independence; give him regular pocket money, and stick to the agreed amount

• encourage planning skills; if you're planning an outing, as a fun project ask him to find out opening times and costs; give him a budget and sole charge of the family kitty for the day

• you can start early by leaving him to put on his shoes, wash his own face, get his things ready for school, and so on

• be sure that you are doing enough for him in other ways so that he knows you still care

Teachers

• make sure you inform parents of the educational spin-offs of self-reliance – that children who can look after themselves are also successful learners

• don't be tempted to let boys off the hook because they are inclined to be less organised

• boys who live between two sets of parents may have difficulty remembering to bring in their books, especially early on; it's better to give a boy two sets than to scold him and add to his problems

• promote the use of planners and homework diaries

• address time-management, work and planning skills

85 Let him say no

Self-esteem gives boys the power to say an emphatic 'No!' – to their friends, or to an adult who is behaving in a frightening or strange way. Boys who are expected to be 'good' all the time, and who need to please someone in order to feel accepted, will find it much harder to withdraw from potential danger when this may involve being teased, told off or cold-shouldered.

Sound self-confidence is one route to staying safe, and parents and other carers will therefore need to nurture self-esteem as the core of confidence. But boys will also need a bit of practice. They can't turn from habitual 'yes' boys into fierce 'no' boys in one leap. Many parents may feel, not without reason, that their sons are already too cheeky and need no further encouragement. But insolence isn't quite what is required. The right preparation includes being given the freedom to disagree; being able to to stand up for themselves with reasoned arguments, not fists; and learning to respect their own judgement.

Parents

• avoid telling your son off for having views that differ from your own, so that he feels confident about being in a minority of one if necessary

• allow him to express his feelings; if it's OK to feel angry, sad or excited at home, it will be easier for him to respond honestly and decisively in potentially dangerous situations

• let him know that you trust his judgement

• listen to him properly when he wants to tell you something

• respect his choice of friends; criticise them too often and he's more likely to ignore your reservations about serious issues

Teachers

• our economy, and therefore our education, are changing radically; employers no longer need or want armies of automatons or lemmings; ritual obedience is out of date, though respect certainly isn't; older children, especially, must be given the space to disagree within boundaries of mutual respect

• listen; respect a boy's right to see things differently and say so, provided he is polite; listening doesn't mean that you have given in to him

• explore the scope for compromise; he may have a good case, which can be answered in another way

86 Teach coping and survival skills

The best way to learn to manage some problems is through experience. Experience lessens fear and also helps to build common sense. Hiding from fears makes them grow. Staying indoors or in a car does not build life or street skills, and wrapping boys, or girls, in cotton wool is not responsible parenting. Getting out and about together, walking, cycling and going on public transport teach road and geographical sense and street awareness; going out for night walks will help your son to respect, but not not fear, the dark.

Staying indoors most of the time does not encourage physical fitness either. The two best defences against bullying and other dangers are strong bodies and inner confidence. When boys are fit, and able to rely on their natural physical strength, it helps them not only to run away or wriggle free but also to feel confident and come across to others as someone with whom it could be a mistake to tangle.

Discuss different ways of coping with such situations with your son, including how to reduce risk and protect himself.

Parents

- useful risk-reducing strategies include: stay in public view and populated places; avoid back stairs and subways; go out in a group (preferably with people you know and trust) and stay in it; carry money safely – a small amount in a purse and the rest elsewhere

- practise verbal responses too; a sharp word delivered quickly is safer than a punch

- ask if he's worried about anything, and discuss it

- it's important that he feels confident; don't dent his confidence by raising the spectre of disaster

- if he's going out drinking, give him a good meal first

Teachers

- if it is practical, organise a termly 'walk-to-school' day or week

- include safety and survival issues in PSE lessons, but keep all discussions as positive as possible: fear of 'stranger danger' can get out of hand and undermine children's confidence

87 Enter the no-go areas

Sex, alcohol and, increasingly, drugs in every form are inevitable features of growing up for our sons. These topics should not be allowed to become no-go areas in your family. Although boys need their private space as they enter their teens and will defend this (sometimes aggressively) against parental intrusion and, although it's hard to hit the right note and avoid sounding uncomfortable, it is important to keep talking. Communication must be maintained in case serious problems arise.

Boys have a tendency to boast, exaggerate and fabricate to gain status and attention. When friends begin to boast, a boy will feel under pressure to claim that he, too, has 'been there and done that'. But the reality is that he will almost certainly experiment. By the age of fourteen, one in three boys will have tried drugs. Telling a boy not to do something when peer pressure is strong may not have much impact, but suggesting that he remain in control of and true to himself by doing things only when he feels it's right may give him that ounce of extra courage to say no and stand up for himself.

Parents

* at home, talk openly and comfortably about sex in general conversation, so the subject is not alien

* if talking about sex, alcohol and drugs is difficult, give your son something to read; many leaflets/books are available about safe sex, drinking and drug-taking; your local health centre will help

* be quietly vigilant; inform yourself and watch out for signs of the inappropriate use (too much or at the wrong time) of drugs or alcohol

* if you begin a new relationship during your son's puberty, be aware that he will find the sexual side of it very difficult; be discreet, don't compete

Teachers

* most primary/secondary schools have sex and drugs education programmes within an increasingly coherent PSHE curriculum; a staff member with the right professional and personal skills and knowledge should give this a high profile

* high self-esteem and good social/communication skills are the best defences against premature sexual activity, early pregnancy and drug involvement; all teaching should reflect this

* PSHE teachers should possess excellent group-work skills to enable all students to participate comfortably and confidently in sex and drug education, and should also treat the subject seriously

88 Promote self-direction

People don't resist change; they resist being changed.

One form of independence is self-direction. Children who are self-directed are able to manage tasks and problems independently. They experience autonomy – a degree of control over themselves, being able to influence at least some aspects of their life that are currently important to them. Boys who are given no chance to direct themselves, or who lack the skills or confidence to do so, feel helpless and depend entirely on others to move forward.

Self-direction and independence feed each other. The more self-directed boys are, the better they can manage independence; and the more appropriate independence they have, the more they develop the confidence and skills to become self-directed and self-reliant, and to show initiative and creativity.

A boy's first experience of self-direction will be his mother or carer responding to his basic need for food, warmth, comfort and attention.

Parents

● directive parents create dependency: the more you tell boys what to do, the less competent they feel and the more they need you

● give pocket money as soon as he can manage it, then he can spend without reference to you

● when children feel helpless, they soon feel hopeless

● if you feel he should change something, involve him in deciding when and how; if he wants to change something, co-operate

● to become self-directed, boys need discretionary time; filling his every moment doesn't help

Teachers

● students improve when they have a clear understanding of what to do to make progress; be specific about objectives and targets

● asking a boy: 'Do you want to do this task this way or that way?' helps him to feel he has some control over what he has been asked to do

● once he has a target, ask him how he plans to reach it

● encourage him to think, plan ahead and manage his own time to meet his needs and yours

● encourage self-appraisal as part of the process

CHAPTER 9

Checking Out Your Role and Feelings

This is where we come back to basics. Despite a growing emphasis on the power of genes and the acknowledged pull of the peer group, parents and other key adults are in a strong position to influence how boys turn out and affect the faith a boy has in himself, how competent he feels and thus the overall quality of his self-esteem. A child can be born with a predisposition to be positive about life and himself, or with a negative tendency, and close adults can either build him up or undermine him. Many families contain two male offspring who couldn't be more different from each other. Some boys need a great deal more support than others. It is our role as adults to provide, as far as possible, the conditions within which a boy can feel secure and capable, not uncertain and incapable. He must feel able to influence his life, not merely to react to events and play the victim. He needs values, direction and the capacity to give himself to and enjoy activities, causes and people, not to be rootless, isolated or completely self-centred.

We can influence, but cannot always be in control or even manage our own behaviour as we would wish. Outside factors intervene, and stress, uncertainty and change impair our ability to be as effective as we need to be. Frequently, a boy's behaviour will test us to our limits. He contributes to the relationship dynamic too, and, as he approaches adulthood, he is increasingly accountable for his own behaviour. If we have provided most of the basics, accepted his imperfections as well as our own and demonstrated our overall commitment in a way that satisfies him, we are giving him a firm foundation on which he can build.

Our feelings, hopes and fears about ourselves and our children inevitably colour what we say and do. No human being is saintly enough to put others' interests constantly before their own. Children demand, and need, a great deal of time and attention. Giving as much as they sometimes want drains your reserves, so that you may wonder whether anything of yourself remains. If you do not consciously take time to regularly recharge your batteries (to maintain and develop your own self-esteem), you may find yourself putting up protective barriers in a desperate, arbitrary way – holding onto yourself, but also cutting yourself off from your child when he needs you most.

The best way to help your children grow up happy and healthy is to make sure that you also continue to grow and enjoy your life, both within your family and outside it.

89 Cherish and trust yourself

While you are looking after the boys in your care, you must also look after yourself. We don't need to be told that the better we feel about ourselves, the better we cope with challenge and difficulty and the nicer we are towards those we live and work with. We all know this. We know, too, that when we have had a bad day or are very tired, we tend to take our frustrations out on our nearest and dearest. Looking after ourselves is an investment which benefits others, for, when we behave well, we feel positive towards other people and pass on our feelings to them.

It can be hard to trust your competence during every stage that children pass through and with every issue that presents itself. Most parents and carers enjoy certain developmental stages more than others. While teachers can choose whether to teach little ones or older children, parents have no choice: they have to cope throughout. Your uncertainty will be real, but children value firmness. Discuss any problems with partners and friends, carefully review your initial reactions, and if you still feel the same, trust yourself and remain consistent.

Parents

- talk to others; it usually helps

- identify your little luxury, the thing that calms you down and restores your faith in yourself; it may be reading a trashy book, going to the pictures or having a drink with friends

- make sure your choice of 'pick-me-up' is realistic; when grandiose schemes fail, it can have the opposite effect

- try to arrange for it to happen on a regular basis; while some things can be slotted into small time slots, others need more time and require planning

- 'I've always wanted to...' so do it

Teachers

- trust and believe in yourself; if you doubt your skills, you may interpret difficult behaviour as a personal attack, and react defensively, provocatively and unconstructively

- list what you see as your professional strengths, then identify where there's room for improvement; discuss with colleagues how to share collective skills, to aid professional development

- challenging boys make heavy demands; rather than pretend total competence and suffer, set up a group with supportive colleagues to pool understanding and ideas

- after a bad patch, pamper, don't punish, yourself

90 Let him be different

My father thought I had to be just like him in every way. I had to like and be interested in the same things; he even thought I should be happy to wear his cast-off clothes and listen to his music. Every time I tried to step away, I got the cold shoulder and he got offended. The message was clear: I was only acceptable when I followed his example.

We spend the early years of our child's life treating him as a mirror – looking for ourselves in him. It starts with his face: 'He's got my eyes/his dad's nose.' It then moves to his likes and dislikes: 'He loves kicking balls, just like I did.' All the similarities are proof that our son is part of and belongs to us – and sharing is fun. So it can come as a shock later on when we are forced to accept that he is different, and may even go out of his way to be so in order to assert his individuality.

If we use our child to validate ourselves, we shackle and stifle him. Growing up is hard enough, but it will be far harder for him if we deny him the right to be different.

Parents

* give him room to be himself; it's your problem, not his, if you feel uncomfortable about him being different

* don't compete with, criticise or ridicule him; every challenge drags him onto your territory and reinforces his view that you think your methods, talents and preferences are better

* getting involved in his school is great, but keep it in balance; all boys need space to be themselves, free from their parent's watchful eye

* show an interest in his choice of music, magazines, games or clothes to validate his choices, even if the current fad is temporary

Teachers

* encourage children to be aware of themselves and their differences

* encourage all children to be tolerant of differences, whether they be different opinions, talents, physical characteristics or races

* vary your teaching methods; the way you feel most comfortable putting information across may not suit the learning styles of all the boys in your class

91 Inspect your expectations

Every family has its own history, or story. This influences what we expect for ourselves and those we live with, whether we want it to or not. There is usually a hidden agenda, which children eventually detect and react to.

These days, while we accept that education and careers are important for girls, boys still tend to carry a heavier burden of career expectation: 'I expect you'll be a lawyer like me' or 'You should do what I've done; it's seen me OK.' At the other end of the spectrum, if men in a family have a history of being unreliable carers or breadwinners, there may be low expectations for the latest generation of males.

Some typical 'stories' that may influence expectations include: 'Do as I say, not as I did' (you threw away the opportunities you had, and you don't want your son to do the same); 'Symbol of success' (you are a success in your field, and his success will be another feather in your cap); and 'Missed opportunities' (you want your son to do what you always wanted to but couldn't).

Parents

• list the expectations you have for your son, be honest about why you hold these, and think of the possible positive and negative consequences for him of each one

• think about sport, music, art, school, career, hobbies and leisure, and whether your expectations are high, medium or low for each one; if there are lots of 'highs', think again

• ask him whether he agrees with your targets and whether he feels he can, or knows how to, meet them

• look at whether your short-term academic expectations are realistic, and how you will feel if he fails to meet them

Teachers

• boys need high, but achievable, short-term goals; ensure that your personal goals and school targets don't impose undue pressure on your students

• help boys to define their own expectations, and step in only if they have misjudged things seriously positively or negatively

92 What you expect is what you get

'Time for school in ten minutes. Remember what you need and I'll see you at the front door at a quarter to.' For older boys, this is a far more helpful and positive approach than: 'You've only got ten minutes. Have you got your homework? Have you done your teeth? Don't forget your games kit, and don't be late like yesterday!'

Boys who feel trusted by an adult feel proud of that trust and work at keeping it. Research consistently shows that high expectations produce good results, and low expectations produce poor ones – what you expect is what you get. 'What you expect' in this case is your perception of your child's personality and behaviour. 'What you get' is the behaviour you expect. So if you ask a boy to do something in a way that assumes and expects that he will, you are more likely to get the result you want. The reverse is also true; when you imply that he won't co-operate or succeed at something, he probably won't.

Parents

• remain positive: notice, constantly, the things that he does right; if he fails to do something, restate your request or expectation; don't berate him for his omission

• stop predicting or assuming poor performance or behaviour with phrases such as: 'I expect you'll fail this test, too' or even, 'You will be good, won't you?'

• avoid sticking labels on him, especially negative ones such as 'naughty', 'thief', 'liar' and 'bad'; give him hope and faith in himself

Teachers

• have appropriate and realistic expectations for the content of pupils' work, and high expectations for quality of presentation and punctual delivery

• many boys find it hard to produce neat work, but they won't develop this skill if their gender becomes an excuse; computers can help to improve the look of a boy's work, and encourage him to see himself as capable of high standards

• encourage reflection; this should be demonstrated in written work and class discussion; with this expectation, boys are more likely to develop this important ability

93 Watch your words

Words have enormous power. What parents and teachers say, and how they say it, can have enormous impact. Boys are as susceptible to hurtful words and criticisms as girls, despite any pretence they make of being tough and immune to insult.

Without realising it, we can say things that humiliate boys and damage their self-belief and self-respect. Fathers and father figures, especially, are prone to engage in playful, teasing banter with their sons that includes threats, sarcasm and insult. They do this partly because they are uncomfortable with straightforward praise and intimacy, and partly because it makes them feel powerful and superior. However, vulnerable boys will never be certain that no criticism was intended.

If we want relationships with boys that help them to feel loved and cared for, we must make fewer comments and reprimands that undermine them, even in jest.

Parents

• verbal teasing is a form of manipulation that should be used carefully and sparingly

• give plenty of praise and kind words; these won't lead to pride if we teach that 'good at' means 'different from', not 'better than'

• be aware that when we put our children down, it can be a defence mechanism to protect our own sense of inadequacy

• comments like: 'I can't take you anywhere', 'I don't care what you think', 'What's so good about that?', 'You'll probably end up in prison' and 'You'll never learn' will systematically destroy a boy's self-esteem and self-belief

Teachers

• be positive at all times; sparring with a confident, cheeky lad may be acceptable for him, but may frighten another boy into silence

• research has shown that confident five-year-olds entering school can become unsure of themselves and develop 'learned helplessness' when subjected to constant criticism and negative comments about their work and play

• boys generally prefer to be active and doing, find listening harder and are less sophisticated at managing social encounters and group discussion than girls; tailor your comments accordingly

94 Loosen the straitjacket

Why are you always so lazy and messy? Why can't you be tidy like your sister? She just gets on and puts her things away with no arguments. You're just like your father!

Straitjackets are statements about a person that lock him into a role and deny him any possibility of being different. 'You always...', 'You are just like...', 'You will never...' are typical examples. Everyone develops and changes throughout their lives. It is unfair in the extreme to get fixed ideas about anyone, especially a child. Straitjackets can encourage a boy to become whatever you tell him he is, because he'll give up trying to be different.

Straitjackets come in two forms: labels, which describe what a boy is and what he is not – 'You are a moron, an idiot', 'You'll never be any good at school', 'Why don't you ever tell the truth/finish anything?' – and other such insulting and hurtful jibes; and comparisons, which measure a boy against someone more favoured – 'Ahmed's much more reliable than you.'

Parents

- try to move from 'Why?' questions to 'I' statements

- 'Why are you...?' accusations are the most insulting, because a boy is forced to acknowledge your description in order to defend himself; 'I find you ... when ...' is more acceptable; it puts the emphasis firmly on your feelings, is specific about the circumstances, and makes clear that he's not always like that

- make a mental or written note of the things your son 'always' does, then be on the look-out for breaks in the pattern and he behaves contrary to expectation

- take 'always' out of your vocabulary

Teachers

- don't compare; when you find yourself teaching another child from the same family, don't mention the talents or failings of one to the other

- try a class activity in which your students discuss different types of insults and the impact they have; blame, sarcasm and ridicule are other forms of put-down that can be considered; get them to practice using 'I' instead

- unbuckle your own straitjacket; teachers can be as guilty as parents of failing to revise their opinions about individual personalities in the face of contrary evidence

95 Model respect for women

The best thing a father or father figure can do for the children in his care is to show love and respect for their mother. This reinforces her authority, strengthens the children's respect for her, and makes them feel secure in themselves and within the family. Crucially, it also models respect for all women.

Boys will do better and do themselves justice if they distance themselves from 'laddish' culture, which tends to reject anything vaguely female or associated with women as weak and inferior.

If we want to encourage boys to develop a more caring image of masculinity, we must show respect for women, including female teachers, and the particular strengths and qualities that women possess. Verbal or physical abuse and violence towards women, especially a boy's mother, is often the single most damaging factor to a boy's self-esteem, mental health and future success in life.

Parents

• don't let your son walk all over you; boys won't learn to respect women if you don't respect yourself; taking time for you and maintaining house rules to protect your interests are marks of self-respect

• earn his respect; if you don't treat others, including absent parents, with due respect, he may lose his respect for you

• be careful about the tone and content of your casual remarks when watching films or television; many swear words, for example, imply disrespect for others

Teachers

• discuss with colleagues whether you might introduce a sexual harrassment policy in your school; girls should, of course, be prepared to treat boys with the same respect they may wish to receive in return

• gender awareness and equality of respect should apply throughout the whole school and every lesson

96 Don't swamp him with your success

My dad was a successful, self-made man. He did it all on his own and he never let us forget it. He did really well, flashed his money around, and I had no idea how I was going to match up to him, which is what he expected. I was terrified when I left school and the future stared me in the face.

It's surprising how many boys follow in their successful mother's or father's footsteps and do as well, if not better, in the same career. But for every success story, there will be another in which the son opts out because he feels he can't compete. The danger comes when a parent's sense of self-worth is based on his or her success. When you flaunt your own success, because you see it as the only way to gain acceptability, you force your values and your view of the world onto your son. He may have different attitudes and interests.

Parents

* manage your success with modesty and sensitivity; show that you regard it as a result of your interest, commitment and hard work, not your brilliance – and keep it as your thing, not his

* your success will be evident even if you don't trumpet it; you'll still be a good role model

* don't seek to excel at every activity; doing something well enough, without comment, and showing that you sometimes fail, is a useful example for your son

* two successful parents operating in different fields make it harder for a boy to find his own niche, so that it is even more important to value the things he likes and does well

Teachers

* when a boy is struggling with something he finds difficult, it won't help him to show how easy it is by racing through a repeated explanation

* underachieving boys may not feel capable of following in your footsteps (or those of any other role model); explain carefully, therefore, stage by stage, how you reached your present position, to make it appear a manageable goal

97 You bring about that which you fear

My mum was terrified I'd get into drugs. She never trusted me, checked through my things, nosed into where I went and who with and she peered at me constantly. I got so fed up that I went out more, and got in with a crowd that was into drugs.

There's a frightening, almost magnetic, force that seems to operate alongside our fears: the more we want something for our sons, or fear that they will or won't do something, the more we seem to bring about what we don't want by our over-concerned behaviour, which they then react to. If we're afraid a boy's going to grow up naughty, we use harsher punishments, which may encourage him to rebel. If we ban sweets and biscuits from the house, he'll buy them and binge when he can. If we force him to practise his music because he's got the talent to excel, he'll lose his love of it and give up.

The common threads are trust and power. If we have little trust, and we use our power inappropriately to manage our fears, we are more likely to turn them into a reality.

Parents

• identify your fears, if any, and think about whether you handle these in a way that may become achievable

• try to get your fears into perspective; discuss with someone else how real they are, how important it is that your son achieves in the way you wish him to, and, if the 'worst' happened, whether it really would be that terrible

• give him as much scope as possible to manage himself, within guidelines which you set down

• reward the behaviour you want to see, rather than punishing lapses

Teachers

• identify your fears for a particularly difficult class, individual or relationship with a colleague; you may fear being seen as incompetent, disorganised, too harsh, etc.; reflect your responses and endeavour to change the ones you don't like

• think about the fears of the other person or people you have just identified and how might these interplay with your own

• suggest that boys in your class be open about their own fears, in and outside school; they may fear coming across as weak, or a swot; ask how this colours their reactions

98 The more you use it, the more you lose it

I saw a young boy getting bored at the skirt of his mother as she talked with a friend in the street. He decided to run away towards the road, so his mother grabbed him, dragged him back, hit him and resumed her conversation. He did the same again, twice, and so did she. The third time, he ran out into the road, and she hit him harder, several times. The more she hit, the more he chose to flout her authority.

There is an important lesson to learn about power, which is that the more you use it, the more you lose it. Where power is used, or misused, frequently, it tends not to stop children doing something, but to incite them to further challenge. Perhaps children see people with an over-reliance on power as weak underneath, and exploit this weakness. More likely, they resent their inferior skills and position being taken advantage of. Being neither understood nor treated with the respect they deserve, they express their frustration in the only way they can.

Parents

- hitting is not the only power tactic used by parents; threats, bribes, harsh punishments and elaborate reasoning are also used by parents to get their way; children get the measure of these tactics too

- we remain authoritative not through being authoritarian but by continuing to guide, influence, set boundaries for decisions and, sometimes, to direct when necessary

Teachers

- boys are often less biddable than girls and have the confidence to argue and make their point if they feel unfairly treated; if you fail to listen, you could lose in the long term

- lessening your control will not necessarily undermine your authority; put boys more in charge of their own learning, allow them to evaluate their own and each others' work under your guidance, and the potential for destructive, power-based dynamics will be reduced to a minimum

99 Let him grow wings

Independence is a vital and exciting part of growing up for boys. Gaining in competence; meeting challenges and overcoming obstacles; experimenting with risks and different ways of doing things; gaining more control over what happens to him; learning to set his own boundaries are all essential if a boy is to become an independent and responsible adult.

Unfortunately, the world outside the home is seen as an increasingly dangerous place. Naturally, parents are worried about allowing children to play and travel without adult supervision. Instead of encouraging children to go off on their own and experiment, gradually giving them more freedom, they tend to supervise, chaperone, constrain and contain them. Children are driven around by car, and discouraged from playing even in the front garden, let alone in the street or the park. Keeping children safely indoors enables parents to relax. To add virtue to self-interest, they believe that they are doing the best for their child. But learning to manage risk and cope with the unknown increases confidence and is an important life skill. Boys need to grow wings and learn to use them.

Parents

• opportunities to be on his own give him the chance to test himself; without them, he'll find it harder to establish his identity, develop self-esteem, and adjust socially, through finding out how to behave in and belong to bigger groups

• increase his freedom outside the home gradually, and at first insist he remains with older siblings or within the safety of a trustworthy group

• less socially minded boys often pore over maps and timetables; they can satisfy their desire for independence by travelling on local buses for fun

Teachers

• discourage parents from coming to peek at their child through the railings at break-time; if he sees them, he'll feel tied rather than loved

• some children learn to use their wings by trying out different ways of working; treat these respectfully, and be as flexible as possible

• class work in lessons such as Maths or Geography can involve the use of bus and train timetables, which will enhance self-management skills

100 Prove your commitment

Inner strength is built on commitment. Children need to feel they have the commitment of at least one significant adult in order to grow up happy, confident, secure and resilient, and strong enough within themselves to be able to give to others. Birth parents are not the only ones who can offer this. A child who is able to commit to learning and friendships despite distressing personal difficulties usually mentions the commitment of someone who spent time with him, showed interest in the things he did, accepted him as he was and, crucially, was reliable and there for him when he needed support.

Your commitment will help your son to have the confidence to think well of and for himself; to be in a minority of one and take any flak, yet be flexible enough to compromise on issues of lesser importance; to have the strength to hear constructive criticism and not experience every challenge as a personal slight; and to have sufficient curiosity to explore and think ahead so that he gains the necessary foresight, power and will power to determine his future and not be a victim. His self-esteem, happiness and confidence may depend on it.

Parents

• commitment can be proven in many different ways: being interested, cherishing, caring and keeping him safe, offering support, making his birthday special and helping him to make sense of his world

• showing that you think about him when he's not there is important too (e.g., 'I bought your favourite biscuits at the shops today')

• step-parents and partners have to work harder at commitment, particularly when a boy has already been let down

• behaving in a consistent manner, and keeping agreements to call, write or visit, are essential ways to show commitment

Teachers

• be aware that when a boy is going through a tough time personally, especially when he loses a parent or parent figure through death, illness or separation, he will need a clear commitment from someone like you – even though he may doubt and test it to the full

• show your commitment through patience, tolerance and problem-solving with him when he does not behave and achieve as he used to; there may be simple, practical solutions if you look carefully

• never give up on a child; he may give up on himself, but it is your professional and personal responsibility to continue to offer him hope

Reading on ...

Biddulph, Steve *Raising Boys* (Thorsons, 1998)

Burgess, Adrienne *Fatherhood Reclaimed* (Vermilion, 1997)

Canfield, J and Wells, H *100 Ways to Enhance the Self-concept in the Classroom* (Allyn and Bacon, 1976)

Downes, Peter and Bennet, Carey *Help Your Child Through Secondary School* (Hodder and Stoughton, 1997)

Forum on Children and Violence *Towards a Non-violent Society: checkpoints for schools* (1998) [Tel.: 020 7843 6309]

Hartley-Brewer, Elizabeth *Co-operative Kids* (Hartley-Brewer Parenting Projects, 1996)

Hartley-Brewer, Elizabeth *Motivating Your Child* (Vermilion, 1998)

Hartley-Brewer, Elizabeth *Positive Parenting: raising children with self-esteem* (Vermilion 1994)

Hartley-Brewer, Elizabeth *School Matters ... and so do parents!* (Hartley-Brewer Parenting Projects, 1996)

Hartley-Brewer, Elizabeth *Self-esteem for Girls* (Vermilion, 2000)

Kahn, Tim *Bringing up Boys: a parents' guide* (Piccadilly Press, 1998)

Katz, Adrienne et al *The Can-Do Girls: a barometer of change* (Young Voice, 1997) [Fax: 0208 979 2952]

Katz, Adrienne *Leading Lads* (Young Voice, 1998)

Lees, J and Plant, S *The Passport Framework for Personal and Social Development* (Gulbenkian Foundation, 2000)

Lindenfield, G *Confident Children* (Thorsons, 1994)

Noble, Colin and Bradford, Wendy *Getting It Right for Boys ... and Girls* (Routledge, 2000)

Phillips, Angela *The Trouble with Boys* (Pandora, 1993)